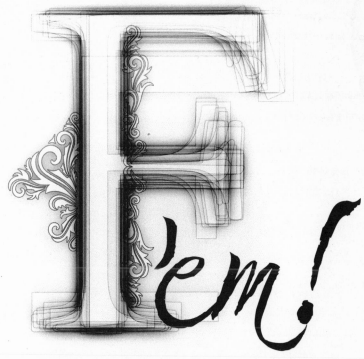

F'em!

GOO GOO, GAGA, AND SOME THOUGHTS ON BALLS

jennifer baumgardner

SEAL PRESS

PRAISE FOR
JENNIFER BAUMGARDNER

"Jennifer Baumgardner is the cultural, historical observer of our generation. My film *The Itty Bitty Titty Committee* was inspired by her uniquely irreverent, boundary-pushing writing."

—Jamie Babbit, director of *But I'm a Cheerleader*

"In *F 'em!*, Jennifer Baumgardner writes about feminism with such unforced panache, it feels as if she's speaking directly, fascinatingly, into the reader's ear. Even the most controversial or erudite subjects are warmly grounded by her sane, candid, witty, intelligent voice. She is a kickass writer."

—Kate Christensen, author of *The Great Man* and *The Astral*

"Feminism is frequently defined in terms of 'waves,' as if women were continually out to sea. I count on feminists like Jennifer Baumgardner to get out of the damned water so that we can finally begin basking in the sun of complete equality."

—Judy Chicago, artist, writer, and educator

"This new collection of essays and interviews by the fearlessly intelligent Jennifer Baumgardner is the book you want to give your sister, your best friend, the college roommate who invited you to your first Take Back the Night and your brother who has two teenage daughters. I hope someone gives it to Hillary Clinton, Huma Abedin, Debbie Wasserman Schultz, and Sarah Palin. The book is called *F 'em*, but the writing gets an A+."

—Veronica Chambers, journalist and author of several books, including *Kickboxing Geishas* and *The Joy of Doing Things Badly*

F'EM!

Goo Goo, Gaga, and Some Thoughts on Balls

Copyright © 2011 by Jennifer Baumgardner

Published by
Seal Press
A Member of the Perseus Books Group
1700 Fourth Street
Berkeley, California

Library of Congress Cataloging-in-Publication Data

Baumgardner, Jennifer, 1970-
   F 'em! : goo goo, gaga, and some thoughts on balls / by Jennifer Baumgardner.
      p. cm.
   ISBN-13: 978-1-58005-360-0
   ISBN-10: 1-58005-360-2
   1. Feminism. 2. Women social reformers. I. Title. II. Title: Feminism.
   HQ1155.B38 2011
   305.42—dc22

                                  2011008282

9 8 7 6 5 4 3 2 1

Cover and interior design by Domini Dragoone
Printed in the United States of America
Distributed by Publishers Group West

For Skuli,
who encapsulated writing and
activism for me when he said,
"I like Silly Putty, but the more
interesting toy is 'Serious Putty.'
Serious Putty is a blank piece of paper."

And for Magnus and BD,
who, with just the right combination of
serious and silly, created the Bedbaums.

CONTENTS

IS THIS WHAT A FEMINIST LOOKS LIKE?

"Is Sarah Palin a feminist?" I asked a group of intelligent, fresh-faced Iowa undergrads, their professors, and assorted locals in the fall of 2010. I was giving a lecture at Cornell College, standing in their commons. "No way!" was the immediate reply from a few, coupled with some hissing. I was game. "Okay, why?" I asked. "What precludes Sarah Palin from being a feminist? Sarah Palin calls herself a feminist, acknowledges that her station in life is in part due to feminist battles fought in the past, and believes women can and should be in positions of power and authority. Her husband is the supporting player in their marriage and doesn't appear emasculated by the role. She has five children, a grandchild, and she works full-time. Is it because she's a Republican?"

No one thought being a Republican meant you couldn't be a feminist.

"She's pro-life," offered one student with long dark hair. "That's my problem with her."

"Do you have to be pro-choice to be a feminist?" I asked.

Some people nodded, but the dark-haired student said, "No. I don't think you do."

"You can be personally pro-life," offered another student, "but you can't pass laws that make it so women can't get abortions." Others nodded.

"But Sarah Palin hasn't done that," I countered, playing the Grizzly Mama's advocate. "She had opportunities as governor to restrict abortion and she didn't take them." We ended up with an awkward consensus that Sarah Palin didn't seem like she could be a feminist, but it was hard to say why.

Lady Gaga was similarly vexing. "She doesn't self-describe as a feminist," said a women's studies professor in the audience, citing a Norwegian interview. "But she does," I challenged, citing several other quotes in the *LA Times, Cosmopolitan*, and *Bust*. "She's self-made, sexual-yet-untethered to one person or gender, writes her own music, makes strange videos that make me think about women and gender and sex, and she is electrifying," I added. After all, Gaga's "Born That Way" anthem helps me get out of a recent neurotic state about my own looks.

IN NEARLY FIFTEEN years of lecturing across the country about feminism, visiting more than 300 colleges, community groups, and high schools, I have learned two things. First: Many, many people relate to its core ideas—egalitarianism, eradicating sexism, and recognizing the historic oppression of women. Second: Most of these same people are very confused about feminism. What does the philosophy mean? Who can be a feminist? What does feminism demand of a person?

Feminism is a belief in the full political, social, and economic equality of all people. This part is uncontroversial to most people I meet because it shares qualities with other widely held belief systems such as democracy, meritocracy, and human rights. Feminism is also a movement to make sure that all people have access to enough information and resources (money, social support) to make authentic decisions about their lives. Thus, it's not the decision one makes so much as the ability to make a decision that indicates whether feminism has arrived in your life. This part of the definition is more controversial because it implies freedom (which people like) but also confounds commonly held assumptions about what makes a decision feminist. Is taking your husband's name anti-feminist? How about having your fourth abortion? In both cases, context is all.

Because some choices have historically been labeled feminist. The Second Wave critiqued institutions that unfairly targeted women, such as marriage, makeup, and domestic labor.

The critiques were designed to unmask the constraints that married life, beauty standards, and housework unfairly placed on women, usually for the benefit of men. This analysis also interrupted the idea that a woman's value was based primarily on her looks and her ability to attract a man who would support her while she did unpaid labor for him. The criticism implied that there were choices that challenged norms, but not that there was a laundry list of automatically feminist decisions. You weren't a feminist simply because you kept your own name, didn't marry, wore hemp clothing, ate vegan, slept only with women, or didn't shave—though certainly you could be a feminist who did those things. In other words, you might be a feminist who wore stilettos, but your shoes neither clinched nor disqualified your membership.

Regardless of one's footwear, a feminist understands and acknowledges the historic oppression of women and the existence of sexism. Sexist assumptions certainly hurt men, but it is women and girls who are more often the victims of laws and norms that hold men above women. A feminist acknowledges this history also but reacts to the conditions of his or her time, taking insight and strategies from the past but not living in it. To live in the past is to ignore the obligations and challenges of the present.

Manifesting feminism in the present is hard work. It means willing it to come into being, in our own lives and in our communities, not by ticking off chores on a feminist to-do list, but by constantly turning the central definition of it over and over in our minds, trying to more deeply understand how to expose and defang sexism. Forty years ago, one feminist task was kicking open doors marked "Men Only." The job of the Third Wave wasn't to keep knocking on that door, but to enter and inhabit the rooms.

The pieces in this book all emanate from feminism—the movement and the sensibility. The book is three equally distributed elements: old, new, and inspiration. The old, reprinted pieces span from when I left *Ms.* magazine (1997), and began writing full time, to the present. During that time, I learned to write the feminist piece for every type of magazine rather than a piece in the (one, often marginalized) feminist magazine. I have been lucky that editors from publications as diverse as *The Nation, Glamour, Harper's Bazaar*, and *Dissent* were interested in my perspective and afforded me a chance to learn and delve into the issues that meant most to me—from abortion to rape to sex to parenting. The new essays in this book represent some of my current thinking about feminism, and I hope provoke debate and spur deeper understanding of what feminism can mean. The inspirational pieces are interviews with some of the most important influences on the Third Wave, and on me. Not Sarah Palin and Lady Gaga, but rebels and intellectuals such as Kathleen Hanna, Julia Serano, and Loretta Ross. These are women who revolutionized my thinking and created the architecture of current feminism.

IN THE LAST decade, I have received dozens of "This Is What A Feminist Looks Like" shirts. It just recently occurred to me that the slogan isn't just to point out that there is no single feminist "look," the line demonstrates that feminists actually look at the world differently. Every morning, we wake up and put on our feminist lenses. These prescription specs enable us to see history with women in it, to reinterpret our present so that women are valued, and to envision a humane and compassionate future.

At the end of this book, I hope you will believe that it is less important for you to figure out if Sarah Palin and Lady Gaga are feminists, and far more crucial to figure out if *you* are. If the answer is yes, how will you marshal your power, skills, and values to make the world a place in which all people matter? What will your feminism look like?

—Jennifer Baumgardner,
New York City, April 2011

THE THIRD WAVE IS 40

"Why do you do that?" asked my twenty-something student Jake in front of the class. Jake wears skinny cobalt jeans, studded Louboutin shoes, and carries a chic man-satchel. "Why do you always joke that you are elderly and 120 years old? It doesn't fit in with the rest of your attitude."

I stammered a bit. "I think it's because of my forehead wrinkles," I said finally, gesturing at the squiggly lines and raising my eyebrows dramatically. "And because forty seems sort of old to me and . . . " I petered out, deflated by how stupid I sounded. Ever since I'd passed thirty-five, I had found myself constantly referring to my age and my geriatric failings. Instead of just asking that my shyer students speak up, I mentioned my bad hearing. I babbled about how out of it I was, how inept at Twitter. I didn't go so far as to suggest the past tense of "tweet" wasn't "tweeted," but "twat," as a Second Wave friend had, but I peppered my conversation with anxious little belches about my advancing age.

It wasn't an expression of the charming self-deprecation I advise my students at The New School to employ to gain the trust of their readers; it was much more awkward than that. On the surface, it was bait—I wanted people to cut me off with a snort and say, "You? You're hardly old! What are you, thirty?" I wasn't reassured when I occasionally got that response, though, because I knew I all but demanded, rather than inspired, the compliment. Jake was right—given my stated values, I shouldn't need this kind of propping up. I wasn't a "do these jeans make my butt look fat?" kind of gal. I was the "let's tell the truth about our vulnerabilities and use this mirror to look at our vulvas" kind. I don't even believe that forty is remotely old, nor do I fear aging. My grandma is 101 and I want to look like her when I'm 90.

Underneath it all, I believe this unfortunate tic is because of feminism—or at least my identity within it. For nearly twenty years, I have described how the world I was raised in differed from that of the Second Wave and how the feminism I practiced was an expression of the trends that shaped my youth. Thus, my mother's generation couldn't play sports; my generation of girls had many opportunities to do so, thanks to Title IX, the 1972 law that ensured equal access to resources in education. Some of these sports-playing girls went on to found the Women's World Cup and the WNBA, something our foremothers could scarcely have imagined.

When it came to sex, we had birth control, sex education, feminist bibles like *Our Bodies, Ourselves,* and legal abortion, not to mention toy stores like Babeland and the expectation that girls have sex, just like boys (though not necessarily *with* boys). My coming-of-age as a feminist began with becoming conscious of the Second Wave, but I wasn't confident about my views and my identity as a feminist until I discovered and aligned with my own peers.

I remember very clearly those first heady days when I began to see what we Third Wavers were doing right. We came into focus one day, and I could suddenly see that we were all over the place, making change and evolving feminism. One snapshot: I read Nomy Lamm's zine *I'm So Fucking Beautiful* in 1994 and feel electrified by the marriage of DIY form and radical feminist content. Among many accomplishments, Lamm builds on Susie Orbach's seminal *Fat Is a Feminist Issue*—and introduces me to that Second Wave classic. *Click!* Or: I'm lecturing at a small Midwestern college with Amy Richards just after our book *Manifesta* has come out. The crowd is huge, filled with students, and yet the women's studies professor who is our host stands and says, "Young women today reject feminism." Amy and I smile as a crowd of young women and men stand up to protest the characterization. *Click!* Or: One day in 2003, I interview a woman who says she thinks of her aborted fetus as a baby, and I know, as I didn't the year before, that the feminist thing to do is to listen and learn, not to talk her out of her feelings. *Click!*

These personal clicks came fast and furious. They enabled Amy and me to write *Manifesta,* which was primarily an attempt to document the feminism we saw all around us—the women and men leading feminist lives, even if they didn't call it feminism. While we were basically the same people before *Manifesta* as we were after the book came out, we were treated very differently by many Second Wave feminists. Suddenly, younger women were more visible. The contributions we were making to feminism—our willingness to engage in complicated discussions about rape and abortion and sex work where rhetoric could go only so far—began to look less like backtracking and more like momentum. After all, we were the future. We had inevitability on our side and had even earned some credibility.

Second Wave feminists were still very active and had many important things to do for the movement, and their individual and collective achievements continued to be relevant, effective, inspiring, and vital to women's progress all over the world. On the other hand, they were no longer the ones needing abortions or utilizing current technology. The time had come for those raised on Title IX, Madonna, Riot Grrrls, and Oprah to move the movement.

In college in the early 1990s, I was awakened by the work of Andrea Dworkin and amazed by the antics of the Guerrilla Girls. Still, it wasn't until I read Naomi Wolf's *The Beauty Myth: How Images of Beauty Are Used Against Women*—the 1991 bestseller that people passed around my dorm like pot—that I truly felt spoken to as a young feminist. Several years later, I mentioned how influential Wolf's book was for me to Alix Kates Shulman, a Second Wave friend, over tea. An original Redstocking, a major player in the Miss America protest, and a hugely successful author, Alix arched her lovely eyebrow at me. "*Really?*" she said. "But we [her peers] already wrote all of that theory critiquing beauty standards and how they keep women down in the seventies." It's true, they had. But I hadn't read it until Wolf. And I certainly hadn't received the information in that kind of package. Wolf's voluminous hair, pretty face, and accessible jejuneness had invited me to read the book as much as my interest in feminism had.

"Naomi's a popularizer, I guess," said Alix, after a moment. "We need those people, too."

For me, Wolf, in all her glamour and insight, was soon joined by Rebecca Walker, Kathleen Hanna, Susan Faludi, Amy Richards, Ani DiFranco, Farai Chideya, Ariel Levy, and a whole host of other women who, like I was, were writing and speaking for and about feminists. A critical mass of us emerged, and with that emergence came generational tension characterized by public complaints and private resentments. The Second Wave complaint was that they had gotten there first and were not being acknowledged; furthermore, they were a lot more radical and thus more effective. The Third Wave complained of not being respected by the Second Wave, who seemed preoccupied with asking, "Where are the young feminists?" Yet when all of the Riot Grrrls, *Bust* readers, and Third Wave activists raised our hands to be counted, they somehow couldn't see or recognize us.

As for radicalism, the Third Wave proudly boasted multiple strategies for changing the world, and mass protest was only one of them. We wrote music, TV shows, magazines, and movies, along with important books. We were as interested in creating pop culture as the Second Wave was in critiquing it. The Third Wave incorporated theory from within the Second Wave—from women of color, gay people, and transpeople—into our feminism and their approach to activism. Thus, abortion wasn't the biggest issue, porn wasn't taboo, and women-only spaces were no longer the priority. Some in the Second Wave worried how "big tent" feminism had become. Susan Faludi called this conflict "Feminism's Ritual Matricide" in a 2010 cover story in *Harper's,* writing:

> *With each go-round, women make gains, but the movement never seems able to establish an enduring birthright, a secure line of descent—to reproduce itself as a strong and sturdy force. At the core of America's most fruitful political movement resides a perpetual barrenness.*

While that grudge continued to simmer, we all aged. Since *Manifesta* was published, some women who appear in its pages, such as Andrea Dworkin, Betty Friedan, Marilyn French, Mary Daly, Shirley Chisholm, Barbara Seaman, June Jordan, and Ellen Willis, as well as civil rights icons like Rosa Parks and Coretta Scott King, have all passed. Meanwhile, my peers are in a different stage, too. In our forties now, we are raising children, struggling with infertility, and getting divorced. We're middle-aged.

There is a power in youth. It's partly the energy—I used to be able to stay up all night to have fun or follow through on an idea, and now I'm lucky if make it to midnight. It's also the effortless beauty—the plump cheeks and shiny hair and body that works the best it ever will. But the strength of youth is also being "in it" and "of it," rather than out of it. When Amy and I were promoting *Manifesta,* I knew beyond a shadow of a doubt that my red pleather pants (chic in 2000, I swear) and snug "I Spy Sexism" T-shirt spoke volumes about whether feminism was relevant. My working knowledge of *Buffy the Vampire Slayer* was as important as my having read *The Feminine Mystique.* I addressed crowds of younger women and men at colleges across the country those first few years with Amy, confident that we were speaking as older sisters. "We're here to let you know that feminism is for you," we conveyed with both our friendly talks and our penchant for fishnet stockings, "and *you* are as important to feminism as anything that came before it."

One young woman, Courtney Martin, wrote about our effect on her when she was an undergrad at Barnard, saying that she had been reluctant to call herself a feminist (in spite of deeply held beliefs) because it was too confusingly connected to her mother and another era. "This was contemporary, brash, even a little sexy," Courtney wrote of our presence. "This is who I wanted to be."

Courtney went on to be a core blogger on Feministing, the author of several books, and the founder of the Secret Society for Creative Philanthropy, among many other accomplishments. She's a decade younger than I am, and I can already see a critical mass of her peers having the effect on younger audiences that I once had.

When I address crowds now, I don't dress as zanily as I once did. I'm more likely to wear a blazer than a giant white fake-fur jacket. My remarks are peppered with references to my children and schools and having a mortgage. I attempt to talk about Nicki

Minaj, the young rapper with all the gender-extending alter egos, but I know I'm in danger of sounding out of it (as that description perhaps just exemplified). My memories of college, which I drew from to make connections, are now further away and less relevant to my audience. "We didn't have email or the Internet when I was in college," I might say, and it's sort of like the curfews for women that I used to hear Second Wavers reference—interesting, but alien.

Although I'm in another awkward adolescence, it's not one of youth. (You can tell by the wrinkles that frame the zits.) This crisis is one that Second Wave women had to go through, too, when it became clear that they could no longer speak for the fresh recruits of feminism. Their fall from that rampart was complicated by the backlash of the 1980s, when a slew of pop culture and putative journalism piled on to express a nation's anxiety about independent women, causing them to think it was mainly antifeminist forces pushing them from their spotlight. Those feminists licked their wounds for a while, but then some, like Ann Snitow and Charlotte Bunch, turned their attention internationally. Others, like Marie Wilson and Nancy Gruver, skipped over problematic adults altogether and focused on creating a movement to address girls' self esteem, creating the 1990s phenomena Take Our Daughters to Work Day and *New Moon Magazine*.

And others, like Marcia Ann Gillespie and Winona LaDuke, continued to break barriers for women—becoming the first African American woman to run a "general audience" magazine or the first Native American woman to mount a campaign to become the Vice President of the country.

Still, it was not without resistance that many faced my generation. We heard: "We did that already!" "That's not feminism." "Today's younger women seem to not understand how tenuous their newly won rights are." I found myself in the audience at panels where well-known Second Wavers spoke about my peers, seemingly only to tear us down. I attended meetings where the topic was "What do you young women think about abortion?" and waited in vain for someone to call on any of the young people with their hands raised. Eventually, we started our own organizations, projects, and periodicals. We wrote our own books. We became part of the feminist establishment.

Now it's our turn to feel the pinch of time. I admit I have read a younger feminist's work and said to myself with a mix of alarm and pride, *Amy and I already addressed that in* Manifesta *and* Grassroots! I admit I feel anxious about appearing out of it. I am still confused by Twitter, and I don't think I have time to figure it out, either. I don't speak for the future the way I once did. I still have a lot to do and say for feminism, but I'm not the person who will necessarily make audiences of twenty-year-olds say with excitement, "She's like me. Maybe I'm a feminist, too."

As I shed the skin of "young feminist," though, I find myself a lot more settled about being forty. I am working on more interesting projects than I was ten years ago, from a film about rape to hosting feminist summer camps (cocreated with Amy Richards), and don't feel that I am at all irrelevant. Still, there is this magic about being a "young feminist" that has media currency and offered me a cherished and proud identity for a long time. I hope that I will do a good job of getting myself off the stage and into the audience for panels on "young feminism," so I can learn from the future even as I revere my own feminist past.

I feel smarter than I did as a young feminist, it's true, but the feminists fifteen years younger than I am inspire me. These feminists, raised after the horror of 9/11 and the good intentions of Take Our Daughters to Work Day, are confident and evolved, and they do things I'm still reminding myself to do. There's Constance

DeCherney, who bravely asks for raises and never went through a phase where she felt she had to reject style to be serious. ("My specialties are abortion and fashion," she told me.) There's Shelby Knox, who is coming up with newer ways of framing feminism that challenge me to reassess my own. And Nancy Redd, who updated Naomi Wolf's update of Second Wave beauty-image theory with *Body Drama*—a book that features photos of many vulvas, something more liberating to witness than I could have dreamed, even as a proud owner of *Our Bodies, Ourselves.*

Amid these progressive takes on vulvas, negotiating raises, and constantly changing ways of doing feminism, I'm also struck by how much the young fems have to go through the same trials that the Third Wave—and the Second Wave—went through, too. Sexual assault is still rampant, confusion (and humiliation) about how to have an orgasm abounds, and saying, "I had an abortion" is still as risky as it is empowering. I can't save younger feminists from any of this, but as they grow themselves up, my generation can be the allies we always wanted for ourselves. That alone is progress.

THAT SEVENTIES SHOW

On a blustery day in April 2002, I sat in Barnard College's Altschul Hall among fifty accomplished feminists in their fifties and sixties, ten or so students, and two high schoolers for the annual Veteran Feminists of America meeting. Part conference and part awards ceremony, the event is a look back at the early days of the modern women's movement, starring the women who led the charge of the Second Wave. Feminine-mystique buster Betty Friedan was there, as was "zipless fuck" creator Erica Jong. Different-voice researcher Carol Gilligan stopped in for the dinner to receive her medal. Seven of the original thirteen *Our Bodies, Ourselves* collective stood with their arms around each other on the dais, recalling the days when they sat at a kitchen table hammering out the original feminist health bible. Many of the women at the event spoke of having been through hell and euphoria, having known intense excitement and bravery and loss, which is why they use the somewhat tongue-in-cheek term "veteran," connoting one who served in a war, instead of the less bloody-sounding "pioneer" or "trailblazer" or (ahem) "fore-mother." In other words, these women enlisted in the revolution, and they have the scars to prove they were there.

I have attended this meeting for the last four years as a guest of Barbara Seaman, who wrote *The Doctors' Case Against the Pill* and *Free and Female,* among other influential books. I'm not a pioneer of the Second Wave but a person who was raised with the benefits of that surge of feminist activism. This year was a salute to the writers of the movement, and at the nonfiction panel it was suggested that no big, groundbreaking feminist books were being written today. Susan Brownmiller, author of *Against Our Will* and *In Our Time,* argued that this was because so much was unearthed by the Second Wave that it was next to impossible to find a hot, profound topic that would make millions of women exclaim, "Wait, she's writing about me!" Letty Cottin Pogrebin, a former editor of *Ms.* magazine and cocreator of the game-changing children's book *Free to Be . . . You and Me,* added that it was also due to the kind of feminism practiced by the daughters of the Second Wave, which she characterized as very individualistic, concerned with culture rather than politics. (This was seconded by sister panelists Brownmiller and Phyllis Chesler, author of *Women and Madness* and *Woman's Inhumanity to Woman.*)

The theory that the important books were ones written roughly between 1964 *(The Feminine Mystique)* and 1975 *(Against Our Will)* struck me as provocative and inaccurate. I am the coauthor of two books about the current state of feminism, and the author of two more books along feminist lines, so I have a personal stake in resisting the news that all the important writing has been done. Ironically, I had embarked a few years before on a grand plan to bring out some of the classics of the Second Wave. I focused on out-of-print books that I thought were ignored by the publishing industry and therefore unavailable to my generation. In pitching the Feminist Classics series, I was asked to prove that those important feminist books (written and trumpeted by the vets) were, well . . . relevant.

On a personal level, I wanted some role in preserving the legacy of Second Wave feminism. That compulsion can be traced back to my first job after college, in the editorial department at *Ms.* *Ms.* didn't reflect the feminism I saw in my own life, the prerogative of having been raised in a more liberated time, when groundbreaking acts come from sheer confidence, freedom, and a sense of entitlement and not from consciousness-raising groups, NOW memberships, and mass protests. *Ms.* didn't direct itself to an audience raised with both Maybelline ads and critiques of makeup. Nonetheless, I was fascinated by what I then perceived to be the "real" women's liberationists, and I was in the privileged position of meeting many of these veterans. It was heady stuff.

ONE NIGHT DURING the spring of 1995, I attended a gathering for the writer Susan Swan in a Greenwich Village bar, when I met Karen Durbin, now the film critic for *Elle,* who was part of the later crest of the Second Wave. In 1995, she was the editor in chief (the first and only woman in that job) at the *Village Voice,* the once-influential soapbox for the lefty counterculture. We talked about whether young women really had a grasp of feminism's theory and history. I recall Karen saying something like this: "Look, you've got to read the big books of the Second Wave. Even if you spit 99 percent of them out, reading those books is critical." So Karen wasn't insisting that I swallow everything the '70s feminists came up with. She was suggesting that my generation hadn't read feminism's foundational books and thus was unable to build on them. That was an epiphany.

I started reading: from *Sexual Politics* (Millett) to *Pornography* (Dworkin) to *In A Different Voice* (Gilligan); from *The Doctor's Case Against the Pill* (Seaman) to *Against Our Will* (Brownmiller) to *Vaginal Politics* (Ellen Frankfort). I read the novels (*Burning*

Questions and *Memoirs of an Ex-Prom Queen,* both by Alix Kates Shulman; Marilyn French's *The Women's Room;* Erica Jong's *Fear of Flying*). I bought out-of-print books from street vendors who displayed their wares on card tables on Avenue A. I read the books written *about* the women who jump-started the radical Second Wave, like *Personal Politics* (Sara Evans) and *Daring to Be Bad* (Alice Echols). I organized intergenerational readings and wrote in my magazine articles about events that occurred before I was born. I revisited the Miss America Protest of the late 1960s and the fight over the Equal Rights Amendment, reviewed the twenty-fifth-anniversary edition of *Memoirs of an Ex-Prom Queen,* and wrote about the *SCUM Manifesto.*

Then in 1998, I had the Feminist Classics idea. It seemed like a good idea back then—and deceptively straightforward. I (a twenty-eight-year-old feminist writer) noticed that most of the major classics of the Second Wave were out of print. I was outraged. Would *Das Kapital* ever be remaindered? Does anyone have to scour the Internet to find the speeches of Martin Luther King, Jr.? I would lobby to get these books back in print so my generation could read them and take the revolution to the next level.

"Mary Wollstonecraft wrote the *Vindication of the Rights of Women* in 1792; a few years later it was out of print and, with it, the first challenge—the foundation—of feminist intellectual tradition," began my 1998 proposal to Farrar, Straus and Giroux. "As a writer working on a book about feminism, I don't care if the seminal texts of the Second Wave aren't on lists of influential books— I'd be happy if they were in print. *Sexual Politics* by Kate Millett, *The Female Eunuch* by Germaine Greer, and *The Dialectic of Sex* by Shulamith Firestone are all dead. (And the works of lesser-known influential thinkers such as Ti-Grace Atkinson and Jill Johnston? Forget about it.)"

I approached a dozen younger feminists and asked them to lend quotes to bolster my case. "It's amazing that Firestone took on Marx—how bold," said Kathleen Hanna, a founder of Riot Grrrl and lead singer of Le Tigre. Susan Faludi threw her weight behind the project. "If there is a sense in the industry that younger women wouldn't be influenced by these books," she said, "it's a self-fulfilling prophecy: They certainly won't if the books aren't available."

My agent, also twenty-eight, was eager to help out with what was essentially pro bono work. We approached the editor I was working with on my feminist book (who also happened to be under thirty). She went for it. What happened next was a roller-coaster ride of frustration, leading to what I think of now as "Lessons in Feminism."

LESSON # 1: JUST BECAUSE A WRITER IS A FEMINIST DOESN'T MEAN SHE DOESN'T (OR SHOULDN'T) HAVE AN EGO.

I approached Millett first. She had written an article that year in *On the Issues* about how she couldn't get a teaching job anywhere and almost all her books were out of print, including the 1970 classic *Sexual Politics*. That book was the first major example of something done routinely now: the parsing of a beloved cultural creation for its misogyny. The lens she held up to D. H. Lawrence and Norman Mailer is now almost automatically applied to work from such varied artists as Woody Allen and Eminem.

When we spoke, Millett was interested in my classics proposal but noted again that all her books were out of print. She was sick of being reduced to the first book of her career (her PhD dissertation, for God's sake) and wanted a publisher to commit to doing at least four of her books. I quickly read *Sita, Flying,* and *The Loony Bin*

Trip and made the case to Farrar, Straus and Giroux. They came back with the news that none of the other books were bestsellers, influential, or classics. The idea of getting her masterwork out for my generation wasn't enough inducement for Millett. Though I was disappointed, I could hardly blame her. No points for taking less than you think you deserve.

LESSON #2: JUST BECAUSE A SECOND WAVE FEMINIST IS OLD ENOUGH TO BE MY MOTHER DOESN'T MEAN THAT SHE *IS* MY MOTHER.

My next call was to Shulamith Firestone, who has been very reclusive after her 1970 groundbreaking book, *The Dialectic of Sex*. Like Millett, she wrote her first book at twenty-five and had already founded and left several influential New York feminist groups, such as Redstockings and New York Radical Feminists, by the time it was published. *Dialectic* had a tight, ambitious, radical argument. "The missing link between Marx and Freud" was how it was billed on the back cover. The point of feminism, Firestone argued, was to "overthrow the oldest, most rigid" class system—caste based on sex. The book was a bestseller, but Firestone left the movement soon after it came out and fell off everyone's radar. In 1998, she published a lovely, tiny book of disturbing vignettes about people with mental illnesses, called *Airless Spaces*. She called me when the book came out to see if I would review it. I seized the moment to get her involved in the classics project. After many phone calls with me, my agent, and the editor, in which we agreed to very specific terms (no new introduction, the same artwork as the 1970 edition, no publicity responsibilities on her end), Firestone agreed to participate. My agent negotiated for months to get the rights to *Dialectic* back from William Morrow.

Days before she was to sign the contract, Firestone called and said sorry for the trouble, but she had decided she no longer wanted the book to come out. It hadn't made her life any better when it came out originally, and she didn't want to go through any of that shit again. ("Refusing a career as a professional feminist, Shulamith Firestone found herself in an 'airless space,' approximately since the publication of her first book *The Dialectic of Sex*," reads the back cover of *Airless Spaces*.) I sputtered something about how my generation should have access to the book, that it could change lives and consciousness, and didn't she care about that?

No, frankly, she didn't. "If your generation really wants it, there are a few old copies available on Amazon.com," she said. "I don't feel a responsibility to bring out the book just because you want it. I'm very sorry."

There had been so much back and forth, months and months of negotiating these tricky concessions, hours of phone calls, and then *poof!* It was over. I couldn't believe that I thought it was the patriarchal publishing industry keeping these books out of younger feminists' hands when, in a way, it was the authors themselves. As I came to terms with the fact that my vision for a series of feminist classics wasn't going to be realized, I started to see the lesson in Firestone's actions. Her book was a challenge to the inevitability of the female role, especially that of the mother who has to forgo her own needs by constantly privileging the needs of her progeny. It's true that men spend significant amounts of time mentoring other men—it's the positive side of the old boys' network—but men don't feel that they owe other men this. With women, perhaps because we've only recently entered the public sphere, there is a sense that mentoring and torch passing steal from one's own hard-won store of power.

LESSON #3: DO IT YOURSELF.

By saying that she wasn't going to give me or my generation any intellectual nourishment—what I perceived as our inheritance, our due—Firestone spurred me to look at myself and my own book to fill that role. The book I was writing with Amy Richards, *Manifesta: Young Women, Feminism and the Future,* would have to be an "important feminist book" if I thought the world needed such work so badly.

LESSON #4: FEMINISM MEANS REJECTING RECEIVED WISDOM.

Which brings me to the challenge implied by the Veteran Feminists panel: Are today's feminist books important? Obviously, I think so. And although we may not be writing the "first" book about rape or the "first" nonsexist children's book, we are writing the books taught in women's studies programs across the nation. We are writing the books (and zines and songs) that inspire girls and women and guys to say, "I didn't realize that I was a feminist until I read your book" (or zine or song, and so on). We are, most critically, writing the first feminist books written by people raised with feminism "in the water," as we argue in *Manifesta.*

Amy and I sought to describe the feminism we saw every day in our peers. In doing so, we had to shake off the received wisdom of current feminism. We had to discard the idea that the only important books were "radical" ones in which patriarchy was the problem, where women defining themselves as a "class" was the clear solution. We had to repudiate the myth that younger people rejected feminism itself, and point out that they (we) may be rejecting a definition of feminism coined in another time.

There is clear value in the past—especially the singular history of the Second Wave, when so much changed so rapidly. In a relatively few years, these women went from facing back-alley butchers to creating a movement for legal abortions, from girl writers never getting assignments to important journalists and authors. By the end of the '70s, there were female firefighters and words for—thus acknowledgment of—date rape, sexual harassment, and domestic violence. There was a women's music scene and a national feminist magazine.

But there, I believe, is even more value in the present. *Manifesta* was published in October 2000 and is now taught at hundreds and hundreds of schools, from Harvard to Winona State, from Lynwood Alternative High School in Ohio to McGill University in Canada. There are indeed feminist books published right now (*Slut!, Cunt, Don't Believe the Hype, Listen Up, Black White Jewish, Stiffed, Yell-oh Girls, Harmful to Minors, Body Outlaws, Colonize This!,* and many more) that are relevant to the thousands of men and women taking women's studies courses today.

"I would say any band that's operating today is more important than bands that came before. They're more important because they exist," said Ian MacKaye, the lead singer of Fugazi, in an interview in the Punk Planet anthology *We Owe You Nothing.* Existing feminism is widespread, permeating every corner of the culture and every person in it. More people identify with feminist values than did thirty years ago. Furthermore, young people today (male and female) have grown up in a more feminist environment. People live feminist lives without knowing the label—women run marathons and universities, men are stay-at-home dads. Given this, those wise words from Karen Durbin can be turned back on the Second Wave: Read our books and participate in our events. Even if you spit out 99 percent of it, reading the books and understanding what younger feminists are doing is a feminist act.

The much-lamented and longed-for radical movement was

both a boon and a curse for writing, by the way. In the '70s, radical feminists regarded writers—even the important ones—as "ripping off the movement," as Alix Kates Shulman reminded everyone when she received her medal at the VFA event. The ideas were the movement's; any attempt to sign one's own name was an act of unforgivable egotism. Writers were the mercenaries in this revolutionary war, fighting by writing, simply in order to make a buck or forge a male-identified career. A writer has to write, though, and she'll do it even if she's misunderstood or maligned. As the women at VFA kept saying, the feminist writer's job is to tell the truth. Those women, writing in a different time, were also writing to answer an ignorant question posed by their male colleagues: "Why are there so few great women writers?" Their answer to that bit of received wisdom was a flood of work and a call to sexist, patriarchal society to open its damn eyes.

LESSON #5: YOU CAN'T ALWAYS GET WHAT YOU WANT, BUT SOMETIMES YOU CAN.

Coming full circle, the Feminist Classics series actually worked out. We had hesitated about approaching Germaine Greer, certain that she would say no because of a somewhat nasty biography of her published by a subsidiary of Farrar, Straus and Giroux, but she agreed to let us bring out *The Female Eunuch*. It appeared in March 2002. Around the same time, Firestone called to say she had changed her mind. She wanted *The Dialectic of Sex* to be available after all.

IN THE YEARS since I initiated the Feminist Classics series, my opinion about the enterprise has evolved. I still believe the books deserve to be in print—but not because they are more important than the books written by my peers. I believe in the series for the sake of parity. Every movement has its classic texts. We deserve access to ours.

—Originally published in *Dissent,* spring 2002

EPILOGUE

In the decade since this piece was published, we've come out with only one more feminist classic, the novel *Memoirs of an Ex-Prom Queen,* by Alix Kates Shulman. The book is wonderful and still widely read and relevant, despite its being forty years old. The need for the Feminist Classics project has diminished a bit during this transition in publishing. Shulamith Firestone's contention that her book is findable if someone wants to find it is more true than it was then. Still, women's history—and particularly the stories and contributions of the Second Wave—are not embedded in American history classes the way the stories of other movements are. I am constantly inspired by how daring, smart, and liberated younger people are and at the same time baffled that there is almost no common understanding of feminist history. Women and women's achievements continue to be erased from the history taught in our schools.

So, to echo Karen Durbin, one of the ways to combat that erasure is to educate oneself and to read the books that came before—not all of them, but an array—and get a sense of the figures and the times. If I became school's chancellor at Feminist Fantasy Camp, I would recommend the following reading list as a great start:

The Mermaid and the Minotaur, by Dorothy Dinnerstein
The Dialectic of Sex, by Shulamith Firestone
Daring to Be Bad, by Alice Echols

Fear of Flying, by Erica Jong
Ain't I a Woman, by bell hooks
Killing the Black Body, by Dorothy Roberts
Backlash, by Susan Faludi
The Girls Who Went Away, by Ann Fessler
Manifesta, by Jennifer Baumgardner and Amy Richards
Push, by Sapphire
When Chickenheads Come Home to Roost, by Joan Morgan

The best part of being a feminist is that we don't have to wait for others to tell us what is important or valuable—we figure it out ourselves. I imagine you will make your own list of great feminist books, send that list to friends, and anoint them classics. For that list of books to grow, evolve, and continue to be passed around is the best possible legacy for the Feminist Classics series. It transforms an individual's passionate endeavor into a chain letter for feminist consciousness.

WOMYN'S MUSIC 101

The feminist historian Gerda Lerner once said that the only continuous thread in women's history is that it is constantly lost and recovered, lost and recovered. Therefore, it always seems as if big leaps for women's rights sprung fully formed, like Athena, out of the head of some daddy figure who got there first, and with no connection to the radical women who laid the groundwork. Witness the Second Wave: In the late 1960s, many of the women who became the leaders of feminism were rooted in male-led civil rights and Students for a Democratic Society movements. They honed their revolutionary skills while getting sexually harassed and confined to coffee-girl and typing duty. Still, they initially felt no relationship to the bluestockings, the radical suffragists who marched for their rights one hundred years earlier, decked out in hideously unfashionable legwear.

But then they got it. By 1968, women's liberationists like Shulamith Firestone decried the "fifty years of ridicule," the scorn heaped on those brave women before anyone picked up their torch. These women turned their raised consciousness and organizing skills away from SDS and SNCC and toward an independent movement for women's liberation. Soon, Shulamith Firestone and others, like Ellen Willis, Kathie Sarachild, and Alix Kates Shulman created the Redstockings, a radical feminist group that paid homage to the First Wave bluestockings (an epithet hurled at early feminists). The name also incorporated a political experience that those women shared—being red diaper babies, the children of communist or communist-leaning radical parents.

Flash forward: It's 1999, and the fear of being called a bluestocking has been replaced by the Second Wave progeny's distrust of being a (hairy, humorless, possibly gay) "feminist." Similarly, among female recording artists in a male-dominated business, there is the terror of having one's work labeled "women's music," and thus binned with records by "cheesy singer-songwriters" of the 1970s, who, the stereotype goes, played kumbaya folk while wearing overalls, smocks, and terrible bi-level haircuts. So, to elaborate on the insight of Gerda Lerner, another distinguishing feature of women's history is that the fear of being identified as "dorky" or "gay" precipitates our dropping the reins on huge chunks of history.

So, twenty years before Lilith Fair was a twinkle in the founder, Sarah McLachlan's, eye, the Michigan Womyn's Music Festival was bringing female acts, all the way down to the bands and crew, to a female audience. Three years before Michigan put the "y" in a word that didn't know it needed one, there was a Y chromosome–free music festival held annually in Champaign-Urbana. Seventeen years before Ani DiFranco bucked the major labels by starting Righteous Babe, there was Olivia Records. Meanwhile, Olivia was the first indie women's label to train female engineers and producers, but not the first label to be owned by a woman. A quarter century earlier, Mary Lou Williams, a jazz pianist and composer, started Mary Records. You've heard of Lilith Fair and perhaps the fact that women dominated the year before Lilith was founded, but do you know about the radical women who seeded this flower? Let's talk about Ladyslipper, Olivia, Michigan, and Cris Williamson and, while we're at it, Riot Grrrl and Mr. Lady.

IN 1976, FEMINISM had just found its way to a commune in the rural South, and Laurie Fuchs, age twenty-four, was electrified. After attending the women's music festival in Champaign-Urbana, she discovered her outlet. "Someone had gone to a Holly Near concert in Durham and brought an album back. It was the live one, and I wanted it," Fuchs recalls. "But there was no way to get one except from the artist in the lobby. That was distribution at the time."

Pondering this inability to find music by women who weren't the token Joni, Joan, or Judy led to doing some research. As it happened, Fuchs discovered a rich history of women who had taken control of their careers—at least for a time—and an even deeper history of women whose work was lost because it wasn't archived. A major label recorded Melvina Reynolds' music, for example, but then dumped her masters in a vault and never released them—a typical story at the time and even now. Elizabeth Cotton, a maid for the Seeger family, had written "Freight Train," later made famous by Peter, Paul and Mary. When Fuchs, now living in Durham, made visits to the libraries of University of North Carolina and Duke to expand her research, each library had a measly two or three recordings by women—"basically Bessie Smith and that's it"— among thousands and thousands by men. "I had this dawning realization—it wasn't that the history of women's music didn't exist," says Fuchs. "That history just wasn't documented. So I thought I'd start this tiny little mail-order business and take my table around to local events."

That year, Fuchs created a mail-order catalog devoted to distributing women's music. She realized that Ladyslipper had to function on two levels: uncover the history of women in music and make recordings by female artists available. "When I first started the catalog, I thought I could cover everything recorded by women," says Fuchs, laughing. "In the catalog right now, we run between 1,500 and 2,000 titles—it's more than we find other places, but it doesn't begin to touch the entire body of work." Compared with huge independent distributors like Koch, Ladyslipper is small change, but Fuchs manages to offer the world's most comprehensive annotated catalog of recordings by ladies from all genres— classical women who composed anonymously, world music, punk, and, of course, "women's music."

Women's music is where Fuchs began, distributing releases from a wave of new performers—Alix Dobkin, Ferron, Meg Christian, Cris Williamson—who were making music "for, by, and about women." Better, these women were bucking rules about what they were allowed to look and sound like, and learning how to be engineers, backup musicians, and producers. In short, a coalition of self-determining women in the music industry was being built. All of these new womyn were on indie labels (Women's Wax Works was Alix Dobkin's; Redwood was Holly Near's), but the most influential, quintessential, lesbionic label was Olivia Records.

Olivia, named for a feisty heroine in a pulp novel who fell in love with her headmistress at a French boarding school, was the brainchild of ten radical feminists (Furies and Radicalesbians) living in Washington, D.C. They wanted to create a feminist organization with an economic base so that activists wouldn't burn out or have to go find a "real" job, but they didn't know what this should be. Meanwhile, an unknown singer-songwriter named Cris Williamson came to D.C. to do a show and was shaken to greet three hundred to four hundred women fans. "She became so nonplussed that she forgot the words to her song, and out of the audience came this voice and it was Meg Christian singing it back to her," says Judy Dlugacz, a founder and current owner of Olivia. The next day, on the radio show "Sophie's Parlour," Cris suggested that it would be cool if women had their own label. Olivia was born.

In 1973, the collective put out a 45 with Meg Christian on one side and Cris Williamson on the other. Yoko Ono responded and said that she wanted to do a side project with Olivia, but the collective lovingly declined. "The image that we were projecting was that we had our own music and vision," Dlugacz recalls. "And I think we weren't smart enough at the time to realize that [Yoko] could have been a good thing." Without hooking up with anyone high profile, they made $12,000 with that 45, enough to put out Meg's first record and, soon after, Williamson's—*The Changer and the Changed*.

Changer sold between sixty thousand and eighty thousand copies that first year. To date, Olivia has sold over one million records. (To give you a sense of that accomplishment, indie-label superstar Ani DiFranco's best-selling record sold 240,000 copies.) Williamson's album changed the alternative women's music scene, giving it an economic spine that supported Olivia, Ladyslipper, and countless feminist bookstores. *Changer* enabled them all to grow, connecting women through a record the same way Kate Millett's *Sexual Politics* magnetized political women a few years earlier to begin fighting on their own behalf. In 1973, women's music became a movement.

In 1975, Olivia moved to Los Angeles to be closer to the mainstream music industry and then to Oakland. The remaining five women of the collective, who had been pooling their money and living together for the past seven years, began to disperse. The Reagan-Bush years hit; Olivia stopped putting out new records and performed a series of fifteenth-anniversary concerts in 1988. The two at Carnegie Hall in New York were the largest-grossing concerts at that venue in its history. Still, *The New York Times* barely mentioned the show. Dlugacz, the remaining founder, was tired. Even though Olivia put out world music and salsa records, it was most successful with acoustic solo acts. The folk music that was cutting-edge when she began Olivia was not going to be the music for the next generation of women. "In order to continue, we had to reinvent what we did and how we did it," Dlugacz says. "And it didn't make real sense for us to do that." So Olivia Records became Olivia, the lesbian cruise line, later that year. Meanwhile, Ladyslipper, which had fought for years to have separate bins in record stores for the genre of "women's music," was feeling that innovation backfire. Women's music felt like a ghetto, and even a band as pro-feminist as the Indigo Girls chose not to be distributed by Ladyslipper.

WOMEN'S MUSIC IS usually associated with a certain breed of (white middle-class lesbian) singer-songwriters with a guitar. If untangled from the claws of homophobia and internalized misogyny, the term actually refers not so much to a genre of music as to a consciousness. Laurie Fuchs defines women's music as "self-determined"—female artists taking control of their look, sound, profits, and career. Women's music also means creating a female-focused audience, one in which women can both be the intended beneficiaries of the songs and feel safe to be swept away by the music. At a women's music concert, one perhaps need not worry about getting elbowed in the face by an overzealous mosher or molested by a free-love Woodstock boy.

The sexism in the punk movement—from violent mosh pits to boring guy bands who nonetheless felt entitled to play music—inspired a group of Olympia, Washington, feminists to create the next women's music movement. In 1992, Riot Grrrl seemed to spring out of nowhere, Athena-style again, with the media's discovery of the young punk feminists. In actuality, activists such as Kathleen Hanna and Tobi Vail (from the band Bikini Kill) were not only reacting to a boy-dominated punk scene in Olympia and D.C., but drawing from Second Wave feminist history. Hanna spent an entire semester studying *The Second Sex* in 1989 and worked at a battered-women's shelter by day. Alison Wolfson, who played in Bratmobile, was raised by a lesbian feminist single mother who founded an abortion clinic. By the time Bikini Kill and Bratmobile moved to D.C., they were actively soliciting a women's audience. "I was at the point when we were in Olympia where I didn't even want to go to shows anymore, from getting harassed or guys rubbing up against you, and feeling alienated by some of the music," says Hanna. "I really felt like the music I wanted to make was for women, so we had to make a specific attempt to reach out to them to come to our shows. We had a mailing list and sent postcards to people before we came to different towns: 'Please come and bring friends and as many as you can.'"

A loose network of girl punk bands, zine writers (*Riotgrrrl, Girlgerms, i'm so fucking beautiful,* and *Jigsaw,* to name a mere few), and activists grew out of acts such as Hanna and Vail's. But, true to Gerda Lerner's claim about women's history, by 1994, the media was already declaring Riot Grrrl over and strong women in punk and rock were distinguishing themselves from a label that suddenly felt too restrictive, too white, too trendy, too targeted. It was "women's music" all over again.

"Not wanting to identify with women's music is the same thing as not wanting to call yourself a feminist," says Kaia Wilson, the singer/guitarist for the Butchies, former member of dyke punk band Team Dresch and Adickdid, and owner of Mr. Lady Records and Video (with her girlfriend, video artist Tammy Rae Carland). "There can be really good reasons for not wanting to call yourself a feminist, but most of the time, it's due to misogyny. ['Women's music'] is like saying 'feminist music': strong, women-identified women playing music. That doesn't necessarily fall into a genre but describes the people playing. To me, we are women's music."

Loads of other women are carrying on the spirit, if not the name, of the women's music movement. They own labels, produce shows, and organize mail-order distribution so that girls and women can avoid the macho record-store experience if they so desire. Some focus on producing records by women—such as Tinuviel, who founded the Riot Grrrl label Kill Rock Stars and is now the owner of Boston's Villa Villakula label. As a punk teenager, she always felt intimidated and harassed by the self-perpetuating cool-boy punk scene, especially in record stores. "I decided that instead of limiting myself to a genre, I'd limit myself to a gender," says Tinuviel. "I put out people's first projects and encourage girls to realize their projects. Instead of just saying, 'Oh, I wrote these songs once,' record them."

Tinuviel and some friends put out a zine, *Cakewalk,* in early 1997 that included advice on how to direct one's career and analyzed the politics of being in a band. *Cakewalk* also printed ad hoc archivist Sharon Cheslow's list of women in punk bands between 1975 and 1980. There are hundreds—from the Adverts to White Women.

FOR SOME, HAVING a new generation of woman-centered music, with its own sound and culture, is critical. Amy Ray started her own label, Daemon Records, in 1989, soon after the Indigo Girls were signed to Epic, and uses her major-label career to bankroll the independent community to which she is much more committed. Daemon is a co-op, which means that the artists are obligated to give fifteen hours of work for each record they do. By 1992, Ray, who had resisted what she experienced as a possessive and separatist women's music scene, recognized many of her values being confirmed by Riot Grrrl—from finding a co-op printing company to print your catalog to using a credit union instead of a bank.

"I suddenly felt camaraderie, like, *Oh, there's people out there who want to do these same things,*" says Ray. "And Riot Grrrl influenced me in terms of hiring women employees—with Daemon and Indigo Girls, too. Instead of saying, 'Oh, here's a guitar tech, and he's a man,' we find some women who can do guitar tech and train them."

WHETHER OR NOT women's music moves you, its revolution has had a profound and unacknowledged impact on women in the mainstream. They created a robust production network of music festivals, club shows, and alternative distribution (a tricky and unglamorous part of the biz, which no younger women have attempted to take on[1]), and made concertgoing something that was geared toward a female audience specifically. Artists who happen to be gay or bisexual or didn't look or sound a certain boilerplate way—Ani, Melissa Etheridge, and Tracy Chapman—all had a place from which to enter and an audience of loyal fans from which to draw. The audiences at Lilith are majority female, Lilith grossed $35 million dollars in its first two years, and over the tour's whole life, more than $10 million went to national and local charities—a percentage of ticket sales. "It's a woman's market," says Olivia's Dlugacz, "and that took a lot of work."

Many of the women who have labels know next to nothing about Olivia or Ladyslipper but want the same things: creative control and to not play by someone else's rules. Bettina Richards' ethos for her Chicago label, Thrill Jockey, is complete freedom for the

---

1. The web has drastically changed distribution since this essay was written.

artists and a fifty-fifty profit split. Jane Siberry started Sheeba, her Toronto label, after eight years on Warner Brothers. "The respect factor was the biggest reason for leaving," says Siberry. "As soon as [Warner] said I had to work with an outside producer, I knew that they had no idea what I was trying to do." But independence isn't easy: Siberry runs the enterprise by herself, from shipping to phone duty to bookkeeping. Richards, Tinuviel, and Wilson all have other jobs to pay the bills.

I'm a feminist who was three when Judy Dlugasz and her friends created Olivia Records, and I want to know about the women's music movement because I don't think it's embarrassing or cheesy. I am proud and I know that the women who are making it today owe something to all who came before them: Motown girl groups, Bessie Smith, Joni Mitchell, Chrissie Hynde. It's all part of the same history, but the women's music movement is kept under wraps; we are encouraged to not align ourselves with them, and the divorce from history makes me shudder. I hate it because it's ahistorical and younger women need to have all of the information, all of the examples of changing the system, all of the victories, and all of the mistakes in our memory banks, too, if we want to stop reinventing the wheel.

The disparaged bluestockings eventually got their due when radical foremothers like Shulamith Firestone and Ellen Willis began uncovering the lost history of their bold actions. Paying homage to the nineteenth-century feminists, they named their core group the Redstockings: "red" for revolution, "stockings" for the old suffragists. Riot Grrrl and the greater young punk women's community we associate with it often acknowledge their debt. Bikini Kill recorded with pioneer Joan Jett. Ani DiFranco refused to sign an exclusive distribution deal with Koch, insisting that she be able to sell directly to Ladyslipper and Goldenrod, the two largest women-controlled distributors, because they had supported her career since the beginning. Many women are carrying on the philosophy of self-determining women playing music together. The Indigo Girls joined the tour all four summers the Lilith Fair existed (which, ironically, has more men onstage than women because the backup bands tend to be male) but also organized an alternative all-woman tour called Suffragette Sessions, which drew from diverse genres. The Indigo Girls have toured with women's music star Ferron. Meanwhile, Kaia, who works part-time at Ladyslipper, covered the Cris Williamson song "Shooting Star" on her last Butchies record.

The women at Lilith knew very little about the women's music movement, made clear by the fact that McLachlan claimed that until Lilith, "the summer festivals out there were completely male dominated." This disconnect from history is dangerous. For all of the attention "women in rock" got in 1997 and 1998, by the summer of 1999, immature or misogynist acts such as Limp Bizkit and Eminem were dominating the covers of *Rolling Stone* and *Spin*. It was known and accepted in the industry that commercial/alternative radio was not playing any women. Without the benefit of the history of women's fighting back in the music industry, the gains of these divas were again receding under the tide of backlash. If Lilith were understood as part of a revolt that began with Mary Lou Williams and gained momentum through the women's music movement, Riot Grrrl, and Ani DiFranco, the twin forces of a feminist movement and music would be crashing forward—not drowning.

—Originally published in *Z Magazine* in 1999
and the Ladyslipper catalog

Kathleen Hanna

"REBEL GIRL" WAS THE FIRST BIKINI KILL SONG I EVER

heard. The line "In her kiss, I taste the revolution" was sexy and pro-girl, but it reminded me of a sensation from my past I had never acknowledged because I never knew how. The feeling was that passionate love and connection you feel for a best friend, and the sense of possibility you feel when you are really aligned with another girl. That kind of sisterhood was hard to find, even for my feminist-influenced generation.

Like the women's liberation movement (WLM) of the '60s and '70s, Riot Grrrl had many mothers. These '90s feminists were a loose network of artists, musicians, writers, and activists who were marrying Second Wave theories with punk rock and DIY culture, and birthing one of the first iterations of the Third Wave. Kathleen Hanna, born two months after the 1968 Miss America Pageant Protest that put radical WLM on the map, is the most well-known of the original Riot Grrrls. As the lead singer of Bikini Kill, Hanna used every gig as an opportunity to organize (clipboard in hand, taking names and contact information), cowrote several important zines

(Bikini Kill, Jigsaw), and took on the cli-ched hypermasculinity of punk rock and mosh pits.

Riot Grrrl had at least three revolutionary tenets: demystifying men's activities (playing in bands, being loud) and opening them to women; connecting women and girls who were isolated from each other, via zines and meetings and shows; and a "pro-girl line." That last bit evolved from a signature piece of Second Wave theory. Around 1970, the New York–based feminist group Redstockings and particularly Ellen Willis (the radical feminist rock writer who died in 2006) came up with the "pro-woman line." Established to counter the "prevailing anti-woman line," this theory said that women often acted out of "necessity rather than choice," making the most powerful decisions possible given the context of patriar-chy, misogyny, or sexism. Riot Grrrl's pro-girl line elaborated on that theory by saying that girls, far from being weak, catty, and inferior to boys, were in fact strong and able to align with one another, and had good reasons for their anger, sadness, and occasional failure to thrive. Riot Grrrls brought rape, sexual abuse, incest, violence, sexual double standards, and queer sexuality all out into the open, using the tools of '90s pop culture—music and zines—rather than protests and pamphlets. They wrote epithets like "slut" on their bodies, appropriating a term used as a weapon to keep females in line.

Kathleen Hanna, forty-one at the time of this interview, is two decades older than the fiery Evergreen student who helped unleash Revolution Grrrl style on the backlashed 1990s. She's married to Beastie Boy Adam Horow-itz, planning to adopt, and forming a new band around Julie Ruin, a record and persona she created after Bikini Kill. Leaders, icons, and stars have a palpable quality of specialness, and Kathleen is no exception. There are the qualities that make her media-friendly (she's uncommonly good-looking, has signature style, is comfortable in front of a camera or a crowd), and the qualities that make her a great organizer. Over eighteen years of knowing Kathleen, I've never had a conversation with her that wasn't embroidered with name-dropping obscure books, artists, and people she thinks deserve their due. When I met her in the mid-1990s, she recommended that I buy a copy of *Lesbian Ethics* by Sarah Hoagland. Her plug provoked me to read one of the most revelatory books about feminist theory I've encountered, and I've quoted *Lesbian Ethics* ever since. She connects the rebel girls in her midst—and in doing that, she feeds the revolution.

Kathleen: Hey, do you see those photo booth pictures on the bulletin board? That was from the day I met you at *Ms.* magazine in 1993.

Jennifer: I've thought about that a lot—that you came to New York and sought out the editors of *Ms.* Why did you do it?

K: I was a fan. My mom used to read *Ms.*, and it was the only feminist thing around. In Bikini Kill, I was all bogged down in these stupid indie-rock fragmentary discussions about who's a sellout. Bikini Kill was a lightning rod for people's anger—at women, at themselves, at whatever—and I knew I couldn't be nourished in that community. I thought, *My scene is feminists; I'm going to find them.* So I wrote a fan letter to that band Betty and asked to be on their mailing list. I wanted them to know we're here, and exchange records—just little things like that. I write a lot of fan letters. I'm desperate for connection.

J: Your desperate attempts at connection have paid off, I'd say. You've said that when you were in Bikini Kill, your songs were directed at an anonymous sexist guy.

K: The idea of Bikini Kill was creating a female-gaze scenario—I was singing to men, and women were watching that. We wanted to be feminist heroes for somebody, just like people had been feminist heroes for us. At the end of Bikini Kill, though, I just felt like a big boob that everybody sucked off of, and I was drying out.

J: How would you characterize the narrators and audiences of Julie Ruin and Le Tigre?

K: Julie Ruin helped revitalize me. In Le Tigre, we were preaching to the converted. By then I wondered, *Why am I trying to change the mind of an asshole I don't care about? Why am I inviting assholes to the show, instead of my community?* Also, I really, really, literally did not want to get beat up. Bikini Kill shows were so violent. I realized I didn't want to play that kind of music. I had to have surgery on my vocal chords because I was screaming every night on shitty equipment and not being able to hear myself. I want a sound person; I want to play music that doesn't rely on me screaming. I want to play to audiences who aren't going to beat us up. I started singing songs to the kids who wrote us letters, like "Keep on Living." "Hot Topic" is for the feminist community, thanking women who had come before us and who were still doing great work but were being ignored because they were past their prime.

J: That's your anthem where you name-check everyone from Faith Ringgold to Angela Davis and implore "Don't you stop." I appreciate that you celebrate, educate, and give marching instructions all in one song.

K: I know what it feels like to be like a "has-been" at thirty. My peak was supposedly in the '90s, but it's 2010 and I'm still making work. That's why I say "Don't You Stop" in "Hot Topic." I don't want these women to stop—making art or anything.

J: Let's talk about the Obama and Clinton matchup in 2008. Did that affect you? I was very emotional.

K: I remember being in Union Square and there were forty good-looking, young, hip people handing me Barack Obama literature, and then there was one older woman with a Hillary pamphlet. I couldn't have conversations about it, because if you didn't support Obama, you were deemed a racist. Which I thought was really stupid, because if you supported Obama, did that make you sexist?

I'm not saying that we all didn't grow up with racism and have to work and work to undo our biases, but "you are racist" is something that is used really unproductively towards white feminists sometimes. It's a socially acceptable way to tell a white woman to shut up.

J: Did you see that same issue with Riot Grrrl?

K: Yes, the women of color who were involved are being erased in the histories. It wasn't a white, middle-class movement. I was a figurehead in it, and I'm white and middle class, but there were many women of color who were involved and were pinnacle thinkers. The major thinker behind the whole Riot Grrrl movement is bell hooks. We were just trying to follow the mandate that she set out, which was taking feminist theory and anti-racist theory and changing it into a language that could be absorbed in various places by people who weren't going to college. That's all we did. It wasn't brain surgery.

J: You also got inspiration from books about radical feminists, like Alice Echols' *Daring to Be Bad.* **Do you relate to what happened to them? For instance, the initial power of radical feminism was based on a kind of unity that couldn't hold. People who were charismatic or were natural spokespeople weren't allowed to be spokespeople because the whole enterprise was based on the idea of rejecting hierarchy— thus, everyone speaks or no one speaks.**

K: The women who took over Riot Grrrl after my band went on tour were the "identity politics gone wild" crew. It became a weird, competitive free-for-all for who was the most depressed and beleaguered. Four years later, the new Riot Grrrls who had taken over wrote Mr. Lady [Records] and me this horrible hate mail. It was sent from my PO box that I'd started and had given the girls a key to. It was like getting hate mail from myself.

I really regret not stepping up and saying, "You know, I *am* the leader of this thing." I think I would have been really good at it. If I would have sought out the right mentors and read a couple books about how to run a meeting appropriately, I think I could have done a really fucking good job.

I wish I could have stood up to some of these people who were using language that people had fought and died for about rape, about sexual assault, about racism, in ways that were just crowbars for their own personal power. I wish I had stood up and said, "You're full of shit!" But you couldn't do that back then. If you're anti-hierarchy, how can you walk up to a woman who's completely tearing everyone down and shaming everyone and say, "Get out." Who gives me the authority to do that?

J: Second Wave feminists struggled with how bad it felt to have more than another woman. Once you were conscious about feminism and how wonderful it felt to be connected to other women, it felt really bad to have more money, more attention, more stereotypical beauty—do you remember feeling these things?

K: I did feel bad when we all organized a convention together but it would be written about as if I did it myself. I knew I wasn't responsible for that, because I always gave people credit in interviews. I had my guilty-liberal phase, where I was like, "Yes, please dump a bucket of water all over my shine," but I don't have that much connection with that anymore. I'm charismatic. What am I going to do? At a certain point I realized I was just trying to be a good girl again, and it was exactly what I was trying to get out of before I became a feminist. Trying to say the right thing and do the right thing so that the other feminists would like me.

J: Feminists have reamed me, especially people who are just starting in their careers. I used to be more hurt by it. And now I see it is an evolution of coming into your own and owning your ideas, and you start off by criticizing someone who maybe you see yourself becoming. And then when you achieve more success, suddenly you're really sympathetic with them.

K: That's exactly the process that happened. There were friends of mine who were like, "That's bullshit, that person is full of shit." I was never able to stand up to it, and I think part of it was from my childhood. The scary part to me is people who don't have this super-strong sense of self and aren't able to separate themselves from crazy people . . . does that mean we can't be leaders? We have to show each other the way. I want people who had abusive childhoods to be leaders because they can be the empathetic people they are. I want people who are alcoholics to be leaders. Not George Bush. But I want people who have been through trials and tribulations in their lives to be able to be leaders, because no one had a perfect childhood.

J: This is sort of a fuzzy question, but do you ever think that you were afraid of your own power?

K: I've worried I was going to be assassinated. I was getting so much hate mail from creepy guys and so much anger from Riot Grrrl girls. I feel like the really interesting part of my story, or the story of Bikini Kill, is we were these fuck-ups who lived in a small town. I was addicted to crystal meth in high school. I was a drug dealer and a stripper to make my way through college, yet I ended up being on the cover of *Index Magazine*. That's awesome. Anybody from any place can have a conviction and be really excited about art and work at it with their friends and then do something that will inspire others years later. That's the story, more than "I am this powerful person."

J: Looking at the music industry and independent world today, did you actually make a difference for women—how they're treated, how they're perceived? Or opportunities?

K: Things were definitely better in Le Tigre. The audience was different. There were far more women and queer people at our shows. I get emails from women who are in bands now who say thanks.

I think that women now can decide whether they want to be overtly political or not. That is part of the choice we opened up. We were overtly political because no one else was doing that. Had I had the choice—were there ten bands that were already overtly political—I might not have done it, because I wouldn't have had to.

J: You just talked about the negative thing your childhood gave you, but you seem to be saying it also gave you something. What do you think it gave you?

K: Empathy—and the rage that fueled a lot of my songs. I have never let myself take anything for granted, because I always felt so lucky. In college, I didn't understand people who wouldn't show up for classes. I felt so lucky to be there. Being grateful is a real gift. I have never been bored. I have friends who are like, "I'm bored." I've never been bored.

J: You're planning on adopting a baby. Do you think about what becoming a parent might mean to your ability to do the work that's so important to you?

K: Yeah. I do.

J: Not that you should psych yourself out. I say this from the other side and believe you have nothing to worry about, although I live in a perpetual state of shame and guilt about ignoring my children as well as my work.

K: I just know that I want a child. I've waited for so long—perhaps for too long—because I kept thinking it wasn't a good time; this record is coming out, or I'm dealing with a family thing. Now I don't care what else is going on, as long as I get a healthy baby in my hands. It took me a long time to be able to trust my relationship, but when I think about the work thing, I know I can figure it out. My husband is awesome and I'm completely sure it will be fifty-fifty. I know that if I have something important that I need to do, he'll take care of shit for me.

J: You feel you have a relationship that's egalitarian and mutually supportive?

K: He has bent over backwards to support me in everything that I do. And I couldn't do what I do without him.

J: Was he raised by feminists?

K: He was raised by a single mom. And we've got money. That makes things a hell of a lot easier.

J: Of your accomplishments so far, what makes you most proud?

K: That's such a good one. I guess the music. I'm not necessarily proud of how a lot of it sounds, but I'm proud that we kept going. I'm proud that Bikini Kill was a band for seven years. It's weird how something that was really painful and not fun has created all these benefits for other people—and for me as well. I don't know if anyone would have found Le Tigre if there wasn't Bikini Kill. I'm proud we put those records out at that time, because it wasn't a popular thing to do and we had the guts to do it. Just doing it even though everything was telling us not to *has* had a huge effect. We started this Bikini Kill archive blog, and all these kids who never saw us live, who are in their twenties, are like, "You saved my life" and, "You got me through this horrible situation" and all this stuff. [The songs are] recorded and they're objects and people can access them till the end of time now. A lot of things came together at once to make that [scene] happen, and I'm just proud that I seized the moment and became part of it.

J: When you hear people calling themselves Riot Grrrl feminists now, what do you think?

K: I'm psyched. I'm totally going off topic, but I feel like it. Do you remember the Fugazi song "Suggestion"? When I heard that song, I was like, "Oh my god, men are actually singing about sexual harassment." It meant so much to me. Later, I started thinking, *Wait, why is he singing like he is a woman?* Then I started having all these questions about it. He couldn't sing for me; *I* had to sing for me. Then I wrote songs about sexual harassment from my point of view. I was inspired by them, but I also saw that they couldn't really do [the song justice], but I could. I've tried to sing about racism in a way that's not always been that successful. Now the kids of today can take up that mantle and say, "The way Kathleen did it was kind of gross, so I'm gonna do it like this." But you have to put your neck out, make mistakes, and start a conversation so that people have something to rebel against. You inspire them to write the song that they wish was there.

J: I feel that talking back to texts by writers I respect—like Ariel Levy (*Female Chauvinist Pigs*) or certain pillars of Second Wave feminism—has given birth to some of the clearest writing and thinking I've done. I'm grateful for the chance to build on and respond to what other feminists, male or female, have to say. Okay, last question: What do you think about aging?

K: It's kind of a bummer, just in terms of health things being a bigger deal. The thing about aging is, I feel more in touch with when I was nineteen than ever. I have the same feeling of *who gives a shit?* When you start seeing your own mortality, you're just like, *Why would I want to walk around with my tail between my legs? Or why would I want to hide my ideas, even if they're stupid?* When I was nineteen, I acted like there's only so much time. What are you going to do with it? Are you gonna fuck around and not say what you think, or are you gonna put yourself out there?

—Interviewed on September 10, 2010

FEMINISM IS A FAILURE,
AND OTHER MYTHS

Every few years, feminism gets kicked up to marquee status under the rubric of having failed, like a stain-remover that just didn't do what it promised.

The media story goes like this: Since feminism didn't provide equality, happiness, or the perfect date, women are fleeing the feminist "lifestyle" in droves, taking their husbands' names, kvetching about catching a man, or rushing to show their breasts in a *Girls Gone Wild* video.

You hear about feminism's futility from obvious antifeminists such as Ann Coulter, but you also hear it, more provocatively, from women who aren't raving misogynists, such as Maureen Dowd, whose book of ambivalent observations on the liberated single girl's life has launched some heated conversations. And most poignantly, you hear the feminism-is-a-failure mantra from *New York Magazine* writer Ariel Levy, in her 2005 polemic, *Female Chauvinist Pigs: Women and the Rise of Raunch Culture*, in which she argues that today's women have, in their thongs and stripper-wannabe antics, disappointed feminism.

Full disclosure: Levy refers to me in the book, and dismissively. Still, I was sympathetic, especially at first, to her and Dowd's feminist critiques. I can certainly relate to the fumblings of women as they negotiate their lives and relationships. Feminism has brought much coherence to my life, but in the complicated and often-awkward world of sex and desire, it has proved less useful. If pressed, I'd venture that at least half of my sexual experiences make me cringe when I think about them today. Taking top honors is the many times I made out with female friends in bars when I was in my early twenties, a rite of passage Levy much disdains throughout the book. I'm embarrassed about the kiss-around-the-circles, but if I didn't have those moments, I'm not sure I ever would have found my way to the real long-term relationship I have today. If all my sexual behavior had to be evolved and reciprocal and totally revolutionary before I had it, I'd never have had sex.

Still, Levy accurately points out the continued confusion around feminism and sex. Much as I fought it, though, there was a certain dissonance in my attempt to be a good, actualized feminist and my desire to still get the love and sexual attention I wanted. In college, I partied weekly at the same frats I would denounce in class as the center of date rape and misogyny.

Levy swings hardest at this conflict in her book, arguing that the daughters of feminism's Second Wave are eager to prove how beyond sexism they are, "making sex objects of other women—and of themselves." These women, according to Levy, "think they are being brave . . . and funny" but Levy thinks "the joke is on them."

The book opens with a *Girls Gone Wild* video shoot, which is every bit as awful as you'd imagine. The formula for this reality video cash cow is to station a film crew at spring break locales where the alcohol is plentiful and the girls young, then egg the women on to show their breasts or thong-clad buns or to make out with female friends.

Levy then lists her compendium of raunch: female Olympic athletes posing nude for *Playboy*, the rise in breast implants and "vaginoplasty," and a spate of porn star memoirs, including Jenna Jameson's *How to Make Love Like a Porn Star*. Levy argues that women embracing raunch means women accepting misogyny—a premise that is powerful and, in a way, true. But in exposing the permeation of porn in responsible society, she squashes all public displays of female sexuality into the box marked "objectification."

Female-run "Cake" parties are written off as cheesy fake lesbian performances for men in suits. Young trans men are portrayed as wildly emulating the most crass and immature high school guys. She finds some depressing examples—teen girls using the Internet to post photos of themselves fellating a Swiffer. And while Dowd's assumption is that feminism just isn't sexy, Levy's message seems to be that sex and sexiness can't be used by women—only against them.

Levy is actually taking a strong stance in an old debate for feminists—and her side is what was once called the anti-porn side. One famed example of this debate: On April 24, 1982, Barnard's Center for Research on Women hosted a sexuality conference that soon became infamous within the women's movement.

The radical feminist movement (the women that brought us the word "sexism," protests of Miss America, and changed the culture rapidly between 1968 and 1975) had succumbed to several splits (black-white, gay-straight, etc.) and purges (Gloria Steinem accused of being in the CIA; any good public speaker accused of seeking "male privilege"). A new burning issue had emerged—porn—and feminist thinkers like Andrea Dworkin and Susan Brownmiller had created an organization to oppose it: Women Against Pornography. At the conference, women who believed the anti-porn feminists were censoring sexual freedom clashed with the women who believed we will never know what free female sexuality is as long as there is a base trade in women's flesh. Carol Vance, one of the initiators of the conference, wrote, "As individuals, our personal experience with and attitudes toward sexuality were diverse, but we all felt that this sort of feminist sexual politics was problematic: first because sexuality confronted women with opportunities for pleasure as well as potential for danger."

The battles at this conference—which by all accounts devolved—set the stage for transgenderism, pro-sex feminism, and ongoing fights around whether women can be participants in public sexuality without being victims of it. But Levy doesn't refer to this decades-old conflict. Instead, she writes as if there was once a good, clear feminism, and now there is an army of women who wax every hair on their nether regions in order to take cardio-striptease classes.

Levy writes: "Imagine how Susan Brownmiller must have felt. She had become engaged in the women's liberation movement when it was a unified, sure-footed quest for change, and suddenly she was in a maze of contradictions."

Not exactly true. Brownmiller entered as a writer when the movement was dominated by activists and generated much controversy herself; she was accused of trying to rip off the movement for personal gain. Part of the reason it appeared unified to her is that several of the earliest leaders (notably Shulamith Firestone, the author of *The Dialectic of Sex* and founder of several radical feminist groups) abandoned the movement when latecomers like Brownmiller joined and challenged some of the hegemony.

Unlike Susan Faludi or Naomi Wolf, who critique the way society has dealt with feminism, Levy places most of her blame on women, especially young women. Levy is particularly critical of Cake founders Emily Kramer and Melinda Gallagher, who host women-only parties in attempt to create a space for women to "explore, express, and define sexuality for themselves." Levy writes: "If the whole point is change and redefinition, then I wonder why the Cake imagery is so utterly of a piece with every other bimbo pictorial I've seen in my life." Levy uses the same mudflap-girl imagery on her cover—without any ironic flourish—which leads me to believe that she may suffer from the same conflicts she is so troubled by in others.

While Dowd's book has some feminists of my acquaintance furious ("I don't recognize the world she is describing at all," a 35-year-old editor at the *Washington Post* told me), Levy's is more dangerous. Intentional or not, Levy contributes to that mean finger, pointed only at girls, that says "You *think* you are being sexy, you *think* you're cool and powerful, but you're not. You're a slut and people are making fun of you."

Feminism has given me a powerful lens with which to view the world. What I needed as a young woman, and what I think women need now, are not more critics shaking their fingers, but more models and examples of the free, powerful sexuality that Levy says she advocates.

—Originally published in *Alternet*, November 2005

EPILOGUE

It always feels odd to critique a well-written feminist book, but Ariel Levy's best-selling opus on raunch really got under my skin. I rail against the idea that there was once a pure, better, more unified women's movement (it was just smaller and less diverse), and I hate how much women and girls are punished for having sex that is outside of a pure, good, traditional relationship. Levy's position was a feminist one I recognized and had spent a decade learning how to disagree respectfully with.

I now realize that the impact of the book on me—it made me angry and inspired—is evidence that hers was and is a powerful book. *Female Chauvinist Pigs* is a book that begs a huge question: What would female sexual freedom *really* look like? Would Dionysian rituals like spring break be celebrated or eradicated if women were treated as full human beings? What if they were allowed to assert their sexuality in the truest possible way? I ask myself that question a lot, because it seems like people are great at pointing out all of the ways that female sexual expression is screwed up or inauthentic, but we have very few examples of this vaunted genuine, healthy, feminist-influenced sexuality. We know what incorrect female sexuality is, but what's correct?

Months after this piece ran, I wrote to Levy and we had a truly fun evening of drinks. She was smart, gorgeous, witty, and acerbic—part Fran Lebowitz, part Emmy Rossum. Our grand first meeting remains a great lesson for me: On the flat page, we were opposed; in person, we immediately saw all that we had in common. One profound thing we shared was a deep regard for the feminist movement and all it had wrought. Over the warm buzz of cocktails on a wintry Manhattan night, I realized that Ariel Levy was an ally, even if we didn't think alike. In fact, maybe she's a better ally because of that fact.

SUSTAINABLE FEMINISM

At Q & A's after lectures, beleaguered activists often ask me if I have any tips for avoiding burnout. After all, it can be very demoralizing to be a feminist who is trying to change the world into one that conforms more closely to her ideals. First, there is the political backlash—the foes we oppose, from right-wing ideologues to people who pervert religion to justify prejudice. *Draining*. Then there is the work of activism itself—organizing petitions, protesting, going to meetings, donating one's time and energy. All this work is unpaid (wasn't feminism about getting women paid for their labor?), requires working collaboratively with really opinionated (or hostile) people, and is likely to garner very little acknowledgment, from the media or anyone else.

More over, most social justice campaigns are *long*. That, too, can be undermining. Take civil rights, for instance. Ninety-four years passed between the enactment of the Fifteenth Amendment, which granted free men of color the right to vote, and the Civil Rights Act that began to make good on the claim. Moreover, the victories are often far from solid or unequivocal. *Roe v. Wade* legalized abortion in all cases through the first trimester, yet a slew of restrictions were hurled at women within three years of that historic decision. These restrictions were aimed at the very poor and young women who needed *Roe* most. Lack of access to abortion is almost like not having the right to it at all. All this energy spent, with precious little plugged back into its host, can result in estrangement from the same movement that was once so attractive and inspiring.

I used to recommend that people who spent so much time doing good give themselves a break once in a while. "Go shopping, do yoga, eat junk food, get off the LISTSERV," I'd counsel. But now I think that sustainable feminism—that is, a feminist practice that can be nourished throughout one's life—requires looking beyond some of the more traditional ways of organizing. But before I get to what that looks like, let me tell you a bit about how I became burned out.

Growing up in Fargo, I was proud that my family dinner table was the site of discussions about abortion, gay rights, and the merits of Geraldine Ferraro's nomination for veep. I liked that my parents weren't afraid of controversial issues and that they were, to my mind, on the right side of those issues. Our family was so pro-choice that even my Barbies had abortions.

In college, at Lawrence University, a handful of dramatic actions defined not only my time there but also the trajectory of my life. There was the ongoing conflict I had with a group of philosophy majors who wore clown outfits every day and picked fights about feminism. A typical exchange might include Mark, the goth clown, asking me to explain, using much-bastardized Aristotelian logic, why if a man *could* rape a woman, he shouldn't. I would counter by grabbing a broom and yelling, "Tell me why if I *can* shove this broom up your ass, I shouldn't!"

And then there were the protests, two in particular. The

first was freshman year, against the Sig Ep fraternity for hosting a Rape-a-Theta party. This party involved no more rape than any other party on campus, but the crude title, coupled with the frequency of the real thing on our campus and virtually every other college campus in America, inspired me to employ the Second Wave term "rape culture" for the first time. The Sig Eps assumed everyone knew that by "rape," they meant "party with"; I understood that these guys joked about rape because they weren't afraid of it, the way I was. The protest, which resulted in the fraternity's one-year suspension, certainly ensured that the Sig Eps were afraid of offending feminists, but did it attune them to the contours of rape culture?

The second protest came junior year. We called ourselves the Lawrence Guerilla Theater Collective, and, excited by tales of 1960s radical theater from our drama professor, we posed as terrorists and invaded Downer Commons during dinner on the eve of the first Gulf War. Brandishing realistic-looking prop guns and nylons over our faces, we took hostages, screamed into bullhorns, and destroyed the ice cream sundae bar.

Twenty years later, Rape-a-Theta parties sound tame compared with the 2010 incident of Yale Delta Kappa Epsilons marching through campus, bellowing, "No means yes!" and, "Yes means anal!" (This incident provoked a federal Title IX complaint against Yale in 2011.) Meanwhile, a theatrical terrorist attack sounds unspeakably inappropriate post-9/11. But even in 1990, my strategies—both borrowed from the 1960s and 1970s—had limited effect. They riveted me at the time but all these years later seem as inadequate as wearing a thong to avoid panty lines.

Protests adrenalized me—I felt alive and powerful and righteous—but they didn't have the same effect on the populace I was attempting to educate. In fact, I succeeded more often in alienating people. I raised awareness about the existence of rape and terror, but the protests offered little insight into how to address the issues. After a while, I burned out on protests. Was I becoming—*gasp!*—apathetic?

In fifteen years or so of traveling around giving speeches, I've visited hundreds of schools. At virtually every school, I observe the student body's anxiety about their apathy. They fear that they are not angry enough. They compare themselves with the 1960s, still mythologized as the one time when students were active. The achievement of the 1960s and 1970s did push civil rights and women's rights into the main, taking our society from one of extreme inequality based on race and gender to one of inequality based primarily on class. Still, I question some of the blueprints for change and whether they would be best for the current climate. The job of each generation is to make sense of its own era, to understand what is needed now. The vaunted volatile protest is just one factor—perhaps a very early or immature factor—in movement building, as well as individual growth as an activist. An angry, outraged environment can be powerful and can start a movement—think the Big Bang—but it isn't sustainable. It's too hot and it burns out.

For me, this trajectory played out over the issue of abortion rights. As evidenced by my Barbies' activities. I never knew a time when abortion was illegal. However, I have also never known a time when it wasn't one of the most polarizing issues one could raise in polite company, guaranteed to provoke anger and misunderstanding. After years of doing what I thought was the right thing—escorting, debating, going to marches, quoting Gloria Feldt, writing letters to the editor—I achieved burnout on abortion.

I began to feel frustrated and suspicious of the people on my side; they were as inflexible, it seemed to me suddenly, as the people on the other side. For years I quoted the heads of organizations, but never once did one of them admit that she'd had an abortion herself. It seemed that feminists had gotten away from placing themselves in the issue, even as they advocated loudly for the issue. Abortion rights slogans such as "Keep your laws off our bodies" and "Pro-choice *is* pro family"—once veritable Zen koans of righteousness to me—began to feel hollow and generic. I wondered whether the assumptions I had made for years were even true. *Is* the main thing a woman feels after an abortion relief? *Is* a twenty-week procedure truly the same as an eight-week one? These new feelings disturbed me. Was I secretly pro-life and had just never known it? I decided to stop writing about abortion.

Soon after I burned out on writing about abortion rights, I chanced on a new project that changed my perspective and inspired me in a profound way. While its genesis was pro-choice "propaganda," providing an opportunity for women to say, "I had an abortion; I'm not sorry," it soon evolved into a project where I simply gathered women's stories of their procedures. The goal of the I Had an Abortion Project became to simply listen to hundreds of women tell their abortion stories—no editorializing, no use of terms like "feminist" or "pro-choice." It was just the raw narrative, in all its glorious ambiguity.

Listening served me in several ways. The first was by deepening my understanding of the issues around abortion. For example, while it is true that many women feel relief, it is sometimes followed by confusion, shame, sadness, and guilt. Older women often feel powerless to stand up against the stigma around out-of-wedlock pregnancy; younger women beat themselves up for getting in trouble when they "knew better." But listening helped me to see how crucial it is to tell one's story. Shame is never good for women—and much discrediting is directed at women simply because they have sex and a reproductive system. I began to see that to tell one's story is to rebel against that shame.

In order to draw out these stories, I developed a better ability to communicate, and, most important, I learned how to *tune in,* rather than to convince. Listening to women's, and later men's, abortion stories shifted the issue for me. It was no longer a debate with two intractable sides: right and wrong, black and white. Each story was more complicated than the next, and I found myself having epiphanies about why reproductive freedom is so essential to women's human rights. Not the received wisdom I had inherited simply by being born when I was with the family that I had—this was a comprehension of feminism that I discovered myself. It drew from other's experiences, from history, from my political knowledge, and from my own life as someone for whom two of three pregnancies were unplanned and one ended in abortion. The power of telling stories and speaking personally as the basis for political theory was a revelation to me. I had deployed the phrase "the personal is political" for years, but I felt its potential anew, not merely for consciousness raising (and subconsciousness raising), but for connecting people to form a movement.

Thinking back over my progressive Fargo childhood, I realized that my family supported abortion rights and gay people until the bison came home, but we didn't actually *know* anyone who was gay or who had had an abortion. (In fact, I assumed that no one in Fargo *was* gay or had had an abortion, because wouldn't we be friends with them if they were there?) More accurately, we didn't know that we knew anyone for whom those issues were part of life. There was a gulf between our rhetoric and our reality. Our value system had not been put into action—I'm not sure we knew how to inhabit the political theories we believed. I was politically pro-gay, yet still made homophobic jokes privately, assuming that they affected no one I knew. We claimed we supported abortion rights, but we were unable to signal to women and men who had had abortion experiences that they could reveal themselves safely to us. One of feminism's most penetrating elements is that it is a theory and movement that asks an individual to bring every part of himself or herself into the room—we didn't know how to do that yet.

Social justice has a science to it: The '60s were a Big Bang. Abortion was illegal, contraception was illegal, black people were actively barred from rights of citizenship and living with dignity—or even living. Women were hostages to a single stray sperm, expected to be educated, but not given a chance to apply this education. So, they protested. The people who were excluded kicked doors open. But that way of being an activist is not as germane today. Our job today is less to kick doors open and more to walk into the rooms—which might look like this: picking up the phone at *Ms.* in 1993 and saying yes when a woman in Alabama asked if I could help her find a battered-women's shelter, despite the fact that I didn't really know what I was doing. Or it might look like Audacia, a young activist at the International Women's Health Network, who is also a sex worker rights advocate, who argues that sex work is a labor issue.

Those personal stories of abortion animated the theories and strategies that had become knee-jerk and pro forma to me, but they also forced me to communicate, rather than broadcast. Quiet vulnerable story-telling is how I got my fire back years ago when I lost my will to fight the abortion fight. I continue to protest and organize because those actions are cornerstones of social change, but the conductor of that energy has changed. Now, that current is more often powered by warm, communicative, and sensitive relationships.

At this point, I might even be able to talk with the clowns without my broom.

Debbie Stoller

BUST COFOUNDER AND EDITOR IN CHIEF DEBBIE STOLLER
has the same early trajectory as Camille Paglia, the thorny cultural critic
who cut such a swath in the early '90s. They were both raised in working-
class families with an immigrant parent, attended SUNY Binghamton, and
got their master's and PhDs at Yale University before upsetting the apple
cart of prevailing feminism. Born in Canarsie, Brooklyn, on November 3,
1962, Debbie was the brainy daughter of a domineering dad and a Dutch
housewife mother. Picking up on the changes of the day, Stoller referred to
her friends as "women," rather than girls—as in, "Mom, can I have some
women in my fifth grade over to play dolls?" To a burgeoning child feminist
of the '70s, "girl" was a slight, not a compliment. In high school, her teacher
Ms. Alpern was a feminist and had the kids read Gloria Steinem's "If Men
Could Menstruate." Stoller loved how Steinem used humor to make her
points—and how something as simple as reversing the gender of who was
menstruating made the case against sexism in a way that twenty screeds
never could.

After Yale (master's in psychobiology, PhD in the psychology of women), Stoller held a series of trivial to kind-of-good jobs (she was a great typist) and eventually landed at Nickelodeon as a project manager. Then, in 1993, at the age of thirty-one, she created *Bust* with her friends Marcelle Karp and Laurie Henzel, surreptitiously photocopying them after-hours at Nickelodeon. The magazine, taglined "For Women with Something to Get Off Their Chests," was meant to be pro-woman, like *Ms.*—but funny and sexy.

Stoller would say there is no money in feminism, despite *Bust*'s success. After all, her bestsellers have all been about knitting. The founder of a widely replicated knitting circle in the mid-'90s called Stitch-n-Bitch, which has spun off into cruises and a yarn line, Stoller has added crafts to the pages of *Bust* and supported, even fomented, a crafting resurgence. Both Stoller and *Bust* have had a profound influence on Third Wave feminism, developing and promoting a "girlie feminist" ethos that undergirds any feminist understanding of Lady Gaga or Riot Grrrl.

Stoller self-describes as a cultural feminist. In the 1970s, this meant radical feminists who believed that women had an essentially different nature from men, one that was more peaceful, nurturing, and healthy—what is now often derided as "essentialism." These cultural feminists focused on celebrating the activities traditionally associated with women, whether childbirth, breastfeeding, sewing, or baking bread.

Cultural feminism was often dismissed as apolitical (even destructive, as it seemed to urge women to get back into the kitchen, barefoot and pregnant) and inaccurate. Many Second Wavers aimed to prove that, given the opportunity or necessity, women could do anything men could. Cultural feminism said, "Stop measuring yourself against men; women are good, and women's activities need to be valuable and visible."

Stoller's version of cultural feminism is a bit different than that. She takes Simone de Beauvoir's perspective, believing that differences between men and women are culturally supported. She doesn't so much celebrate female endeavors as ask whether these activities are trivial or, as Steinem suggests with her article about menstruation, only thought of that way because women do them.

"Shouldn't we ask if doing everything men have traditionally done is necessarily *better* than what women have traditionally done?" Debbie says. "Are these things really better, or do we as a culture give them more value because they are male?" Sexism is reproduced not politically or economically so much as by our culture, Debbie would say, so she wants to create a better culture for women. Like Riot Grrrls before her, she believes that women stuff is valuable—and "girl" is indisputably good.

Jennifer: Why fight sexism via culture?
Debbie: Because, in general, the culture devalues everything that women do. My grad school dissertation was about the influence that the media has on women's perception of their own power. I had the choice to go out and teach or actually try to make some different culture for women. I tried to make a magazine that was a girl's-eye view of the world. It's a feminist magazine in that it's rooted in this feminist idea, but it's not really about feminism. It's just an attempt to make something more positive by putting women and their concerns at the center of the world.

Movies are always about a man who did this man thing and he's a man in a manly world. Contrast that with the second *Sex and the City* movie, which was from a woman's perspective. This was a movie about older women who were not particularly gorgeously attractive like we usually see in movies. The *men* were the set dressing in *Sex and the City*. On NPR, I heard one critic complaining that the men in the movie have to be successful and rich to get the attention of . . . Sarah Jessica Parker—and she's not even that pretty. I thought, *Welcome to the world of women watching media.* You have to be as gorgeous as Catherina Zeta Jones to win the love of . . . Michael Douglas?

J: You like Camille Paglia. How does she fit in with your feminism?

D: I love analytical thinkers who come up with new solutions or point out things that we may have taken for granted. I first loved Simone de Beauvoir. Then I thought Camille Paglia was awesome because she's a real shit-stirrer. She truly has a different perspective on certain taken-for-granted feminist paradigms. There's no clear solution to this puzzle of how we become an egalitarian society. You may disagree with Paglia, but she gave a new perspective to add to feminist thinking. Feminism needs that so badly.

J: Camille Paglia is a lesbian. I think that many of the conflicts around being a woman and feminist dissipate when you're a lesbian because—

D: Because you're not trying to figure out a way to be desired by men. Virginie Despentes [the French feminist and creator of the rape revenge film *Baise-Moi*] said it in *King Kong Theory*. She said, "You can't really be a liberated feminist and be straight; as long as you have to interact with men, you're not going to be able to be free of these restrictions of femininity." Once she realized that she was a dyke, she was free from this straitjacket of feminine display that seems necessary to be desirable to men. Okay, I believe her. But what's the solution for straight women? There still has to be a solution.

I was in a hotel recently. At three o'clock in the morning, I woke up to the people next door having sex. Well, I heard the woman. She was like, "Yessss! *Yesssss!*" Someone's been watching *When Harry Met Sally* too much. I was tempted to go next door and knock on the door and say to the guy, "Are you buying this? Because this is ridiculous; nobody orgasms this way." For straight women, even your sexuality and sex are a performance of being desired. There's very little encouragement—maybe none, even—for girls to really figure out what gives them pleasure. I always say that if a guy requires holding a meatball in one hand and a stuffed pony in the other in order to orgasm, he'll make that situation happen. But if a girl needs a little bit more clitoral pressure, she won't ask for it.

J: So true.

D: If you made a graph of who has the most orgasms—like, the most sexually satisfying life—between straight men, gay men, lesbians, and straight women, straight women would be at the bottom. That's a big issue and it is important that we deal with it.

J: I'm with you. Here's another big issue: You had a stay-at-home mom who was a very skilled homemaker. She knew how to sew and bake and crochet. You, in turn, became a leader in a cultural shift that looked at crafts like sewing and knitting as sites of feminist empowerment. You loved that book _Home Comforts_, and you see the value in keeping house. Do you see women claiming homemaking and being stay-at-home in that feminist way that you are describing?

D: I don't have kids and I don't want all the stay-at-home moms to hate me, but I think this is complicated. What's that Allen Ginsberg line, like "I've seen the best minds of my generation . . . ?"

J: Ummmm, "I saw the best minds of my generation ruined . . . "[1]

D: And I've seen the best minds of my generation ruined by being stay-at-home moms. [_Laughs._] Not really, but many of the women I went to school with are now stay-at-home moms. And I think our current idea of stay-at-home mom is really problematic. My mom stayed at home, but she had a

---

1. I won't pretend I came up with the whole line in that moment, but, so you have it, it's the first line of _Howl_ and goes, "I saw the best minds of my generation destroyed by madness, starving hysterical naked . . . "

lot to do. Being a stay-at-home mom was a big job. She had laundry, cooking, shopping, keeping the house clean, and taking care of us. Today's stay-at-home moms—it seems at least like the highly educated ones that I see in my neighborhood in Brooklyn—have made staying home their career. Yet so many of them have cleaning ladies and order out. I see them in restaurants all the time. I see them having breakfast in cafés with their kids, and I can imagine that that's really fun, but if the argument is that being a stay-at-home mom is such a difficult job and is the hardest job you'll ever love and *blah blah blah blah,* why do you have all this time to sit in cafés or blog?

I think stay-at-home parents need to contribute something to the picture. Even if your contribution is saving money for your household because you're doing the laundry, cooking, childcare, and cleaning your own house.

J: That makes sense. But there is something about tedious labor that doesn't mix well with being unpaid. I think working out of the home is important. Being a corporate drone may not be a fulfilling life, but that paycheck can take the sting off of it. It's important to life to find meaningful work. I subscribe to the idea that work for pay is meaningful.

D: Why do you subscribe to that idea?

J: First, because we live in a world where unpaid work does mean unvalued work. Second, I believe in being a productive member of society. Truly being a full-time stay-at-home parent sounds very isolating, which I think is unhealthy. For me, working has, in addition to giving me a paycheck and allowing me to support myself, enabled my creativity and my sense of self to develop—

D: Well, it's enabled your sense of self to develop, I would argue, because that's what our culture values, and so in order to be valued by the culture and also valued by yourself, you sort of have to follow this path of making contributions to the world. But why do you see having a career outside of the home as the only way to be a "productive member of society"? In Holland, the comforts of home, and the housework that goes with it, are revered and are considered very valuable. As a result, women are more fulfilled in that role. There isn't such focus on career, because Holland is a relatively socialist country. Nobody can be really poor, and nobody can get really rich. Basically, everybody is a postal worker and gets good vacations. The whole work culture in the socialist country is different. People are just going to do the bare minimum of what needs to be done.

J: That sounds awful to me.

D: Why stay at work late? Is it really, really so much more fulfilling to work and have that book published and have some people tell you that they really like it than it would be to go away every winter for an entire month or have four months of vacation every year and do that much more living? I think the reason that having that book out there and having people tell you that they think the book is great is more fulfilling because that's what our culture values.

J: Yes, and those books and projects are links with other people and to feminism and a community of like-minded people. Those links then enable me to problem-solve around abortion and rape and queer issues—

D: And that's more fulfilling to you than—

J: Than going on vacation? Yes.

New topic: You and I were on a panel together at which we were asked to comment on whether Third Wave feminism is just as racist as its predecessors. I think we both felt we flunked the question.

D: There is this whole issue in feminism I always find really difficult and touchy. I don't even know if I can broach it. But I feel like trying to struggle for feminism, *just feminism,* is almost impossible, because all of these other causes get placed in front. If you look at the democratic convention from the 1970s, when women agitated for equal rights, then the feminist cause became the lesbian cause. Gay rights are absolutely important to me, but gay rights are not feminism. And neither are civil rights. I mean, these are all important things, but they're not central to feminism. When we are talking about gay people's right to marry, we don't also start talking about women's position in marriages and independence and yada yada yada. When racism is in the news, people don't also start talking about women's rights. Central to feminism is figuring out the inequalities between men and women and how to equalize them. Instead, there is this feminine thing of, "Oh, no. You go ahead. You go ahead of us and we'll just, you know, wait." It's a difficult thing to say, because it sounds like you don't care about other issues—

J: **Not just that you don't care; it's that you don't see that they are completely entangled. You see them as discrete movements?**

D: I do. People say, "But that's just middle-class white women's problems, and working-class women don't have those problems." But I totally disagree. I think that women, whether working class or middle class, get overly sexualized and have their sexual desire placed last. They face all the same cultural forces and the limitations of how our society sees women.

When I was in college, there was a lot of talk about how women of color were never presented as the beauty ideal. Coincidentally, you'd hear how women of color are so much more comfortable with their bodies than white women are. Currently, we have a beauty ideal that is completely based on the ideal woman of color—a large butt and big lips. These are traits that are more common in ethnicities other than white, qualities that white women can't even achieve. There's a lot of corresponding male objectification of women of color. You already are seeing that women and young girls of color are having the same body image issues that white girls have had, because that same lens is pointed at them, whereas they were excluded from it for a while. I see this as a collection of issues and problems that intersect with class and race, but you *can* separate out the particular issues that we *all* face as women.

J: Can you talk about the existence of a Fourth Wave?

D: Yes. I don't see a Fourth Wave yet. There's definitely a younger generation of feminists. The thing to me that defined the Third Wave was a different set of strategies. The First Wave had a particular set of causes. The Second Wave had a new set of causes. The Third Wave pioneered new strategies—using popular culture, since we recognize the importance of that in our lives, and the idea of reclaiming.

J: Right. Reclaiming things like knitting, makeup, and Barbies, and words like "girl" and "slut."

D: I don't yet see new strategies coming out of younger feminists. In fact, what I see a lot in the younger generation is sort of a reversion to the Second Wave.

J: Give me an example.

D: It's about being politicized and not nearly as much reclaiming. Third Wave strategies didn't get that much press, so I don't know if they ever filtered down to a lot of those younger women. When you look at the textbooks that they're reading, I don't know if there's anything Third Wave included. I know that when I see a notice for a feminist lecture series, it's all the usual suspects from the Second Wave.

J: But social networking and different media tools, those don't strike you as an innovation or a strategy?

D: No. I don't see them using those tools to present a different set of ideas or solutions. I think it's great to use new tools. Why wouldn't you? We used zines when desktop publishing became available. I see blogs and Twitter as still just disseminating the same ideas that we've been discussing for, you know, a couple of decades now. New ideas? I don't see that. I think that any new approaches will emanate from issues around transgender—younger people have a lot to say about gender and limitations of gender. Some good solutions could come out of that.

—Interviewed on June 15, 2010

THIS IS WHAT A PATRIARCH LOOKS LIKE

For my entire childhood, my father had a mustache like Isaac's from *The Love Boat.* He looked handsome, but also a little bit menacing. By covering his lips with bushy bristles, he appeared to have only one expression: stern. Unless he was guffawing with laughter, he looked ready to discipline, and I grew up somewhat intimidated by my father and his mirthless, mouthless face.

I also grew up with *Ms.* magazine, *Free to Be . . . You and Me,* Judy Blume books on my bedside table, and Judy Collins records on the stereo. I watched the original *Sesame Street,* the episodes that were so gritty, with a young Jesse Jackson demanding that the child actors repeat after him: "I'm SOMEbody! I may be poor! I may be black! But I am SOMEbody!" The parents of the 1970s appeared to want their kids to have self-esteem, civil rights, and morals. Perhaps they were idealists, or perhaps they thought they themselves were lost causes and wanted to pass the buck of being good people on to their unsuspecting kids. Either way, it wasn't until I entered college in 1988 that I began to truly dig into my political aquarium life.

My college years at Lawrence University in Appleton, Wisconsin, were my first exposure to "-isms": feminism, but also other vocabulary words that described injustices (racism, ableism, sexism, heterosexism, anti-Semitism). Because I was white, middle-class, able-bodied, and straight (or so I thought), I felt awkwardly implicated in many of the bigotries I was studying. I hadn't ever seen myself as racist, didn't want to be, but I believed if I wasn't part of the solution, I was part of the problem (a favorite bumper-sticker–size belief of the time). "If you aren't angry, you aren't paying attention" was a slogan I repeated, as was "Don't ask [insert oppressed group] to educate you! Educate yourself!" These axioms felt true to me but also added to my discomfort and confusion about how to be a good person while at the same time being a de facto oppressor.

That's when "patriarchy"—the term—entered my life. In 1988, male privilege was evident in ways both local (while the three sororities at Lawrence used the community center as their social meeting place, the five fraternities had dedicated houses in which to live and throw "rum and reggae" parties) and national (there were only two women in the Senate). But when I learned the p-word, like magic, I was reprieved of my horrifying privilege. I wasn't the oppressor; I was oppressed! Patriarchy was like Levi's, fit for every occasion. Do you feel silent and shy in class? Well, maybe you are being silenced . . . by PATRIARCHY! Was your best friend roofied and raped? Well, who invites men to violate women and treat them like mere sperm receptacles but PATRIARCHY! Does your boyfriend call you a dumb blond? Do you feel like your essential worth is your looks? Are you afraid to walk home at night? Was your brother sent to Princeton and you to a party school? Who invented marriage? PATRIARCHY!

"Patriarchy" was a word I jammed into a lot of explanations and solutions to problems that were complicated and convoluted back when I was eighteen. If I hated the way my thighs looked, it was because patriarchy benefited from me (and all women) remaining insecure. While I was worrying about whether my butt looked big, men were making more money than women, using that freed-up mental space to compose symphonies and write books. If penises and sex made me anxious, it was because patriarchy propped up the male member to make it seem important, using a system of coercion and rape. I read Susan Brownmiller's *Against Our Will,* in which she argues that rape "is nothing more or less than a conscious process of intimidation by which all men keep all women in a state of fear." Men's lording it over women equaled patriarchy.

I loved Brownmiller's words. They allowed me to see and confront the unhealthy behavior I witnessed in college. I could begin to deal with the fact that three of my five closest friends had been sexually assaulted, or that some frat guys made posters making fun of a girl they deemed homely and plastered them all over campus. I could offer a response to that fellow who, during freshman orientation, was asked to consider what he'd do if he came home and his roommate was kissing another guy, and he said he'd get a gun and shoot him. Feminism gave me a firm, orderly frame for the sometimes messy snapshots of my life.

Of course, patriarchy—that is, the social system defined by powerful males and subordinate females—does play its part in all the problems described above. Women are necessary to all societies, yet are treated as less valuable. They are paid less for their labor, and activities traditionally associated with women (knitting, cooking, child rearing) are demeaned. Women are objectified—i.e. denied autonomy, infantilized, owned by men, treated as interchangeable, violable, and as if without valid feelings (as philosopher Martha

Nussbaum defined this feminist complaint). Women are asked to keep silent about crucial parts of their lives (abortions, rape, incest, miscarriages, etc.). Yes, patriarchy was a scratchy mustache, all right. A mirthless, mouthless face that was still intimidating, but also increasingly open to exposure.

By the time I graduated from college in 1992, many of the signature historical moments that presaged Third Wave feminism had already occurred: the Riot Grrrl conference in D.C. (1992), the Anita Hill–Clarence Thomas hearings (1991), the two marches on Washington to protest the Supreme Court cases that ushered in a rollback of abortion rights (1989 and 1992), and the Rodney King verdict (1992). Each bit of bad news from the front was like a cold shower on the stickiest hot day: I felt awake and hungry and clean. I moved to New York and got a job with *Ms.* magazine (where I could be paid to be outraged by these news events), and patriarchy loomed larger than ever. It was the ghost in our creation myth. The magazine had come into being because *New York* magazine's Clay Felker liked Gloria Steinem so much, he bankrolled the first issue of *Ms.* The feminist answer to *Time* had been owned by men throughout its life, except during a brief moment in the '80s when Australian feminists took over. Ironically, those Aussie ladies were the first and only owners to deem fashion coverage a good idea.

Ms. as a workplace in the 1990s was a cross between fast-paced New York publishing and a hairy, hummus-y separatist commune. The commune side enabled me to become bisexual and fall in love with a *Ms.* intern, and afforded me the opportunity to create a coven with my friend Amy Richards and cast spells while drinking red wine from a communal goblet. The fast-paced side involved producing the magazine, hiring real writers, and attending press conferences and preview screenings of movies. Combining fast-paced and separatist values, we didn't take ads, and underlings like me *loved* to snap that back at unsuspecting underlings from companies calling for our ad rate sheets. "We are ad free," we'd say, smug in our purity and contemptuous of having something as compromising as a revenue stream.

I was again reprieved of privilege; *Ms.* was poor and unglamorous. We helped battered women find shelters while the interns at *Vogue* tottered in their black Prada booties, bringing Anna Wintour coffee. Another opportunity for purity came from the fact that no men worked for us or with us, other than Jimmy, the mail room guy. However, we worked for men. We worked for The Man. In particular, we worked for our owner, Dale Lang.

Lang made his money originally from billboards throughout the Midwest, but went on to buy several feministy women's magazines, including *Working Woman, Working Mother,* and *Sassy.* He was often cash-strapped and making deals, yet he retained a patina of power. He hosted a grand party at the Rainbow Room early in my tenure and got Bill Gates to speak at a luncheon. Even without a mustache, he looked like the patriarchy: old, shortish, with a full head of silver hair, benign smile; and rheumy, unseeing eyes.

By my third year at *Ms.,* publishing was having a pre-Internet crisis. Paper and postage prices were skyrocketing. Editors and art directors were spending hours every week tracking down checks and fielding phone calls from panicked and pissed writers. The printer hadn't been paid; we couldn't use a car service if we worked late (though that was nothing new) or do expenses (ditto). The office-supplies room was down to a cardboard box with pencil stubs and a few reams of graph paper. I had to ask my best friend to get me Post-its, pens, and notebooks from her job at Citibank.

Soon, a few rooked writers began suing in small claims court. It didn't matter if you were famous (Susan Faludi and Rita Mae Brown were stiffed), or had an agent harassing for you, or were not going to make your rent if you didn't get that couple grand—it was an equal-opportunity shaft. By the end of 1996, thirty *Ms.* writers were bringing a fraud suit with the writers' union and Lang owed over $70,000 to the writers alone.[*1] At a new low, *Ms.* spelled "feminism" wrong on the cover of the May/June 1996 issue ("feminisim"). Demoralization had arrived.

Editors trudged along, heads bowed, occasionally calling emergency meetings to make lists of writers in order of how desperately they needed to be paid. I had gone from feeling so proud and free at *Ms.*—who else had a job where she was paid to think about Ani DiFranco?—to feeling a horrible shame and frustration at how powerless we were to solve our own problems. We couldn't get anyone paid, but we also couldn't stop assigning pieces to freelancers (with contracts stating they would be paid), because if the magazine didn't continue, we wouldn't be able to pay anyone. It was a miserable cycle.

Buoyed by the hippie-commune side of *Ms.*—or, you might say, by its faux-utopian side—I suggested at an editorial meeting that we perform a Wiccan ritual to rid ourselves of the patriarchy. I was into Wicca. No one exactly took me up on it, but no one laughed, either. I took that as a sign that it was a good idea. That night, I took a beeswax candle, some crystals, and essential oils over to my girlfriend Anastasia's apartment. We drew a bath and dropped in the oil, and, sitting in the clawfoot tub together, read a spell another friend had written to banish the patriarchy. We lit the candle, which was in the shape of a goddess. When the candle burned down to nothing, it meant we had extinguished the patriarchal spirit.

After about half an hour of sitting in the tub, Anastasia and I began to get pruny and waterlogged. I felt sort of faint and wished the candle would melt faster, but it seemed dangerous to go get

---

1. Lang settled with the writers' union during the fall of 1998 after two years of litigation.

dressed until the patriarchal essence had burned out on its own. Finally, about an hour in, the candle flickered and died, but instead of disappearing, it left a large blob of cellulite-like wax. "What are we supposed to do with the glob?" I asked Anastasia.

"I'm not sure," she said, "but I think we can get out of the tub." We dressed, but I felt anxious when she handed me the glob on my way out the door. "We'll figure out how you dispose of the by-product," she said reassuringly as I left her apartment with the patriarchy in my purse. The next day, she instructed me to hurl the remains into a body of water.

Although Manhattan is an island bordered by two rivers, one of which is a brackish estuary that runs into the Atlantic Ocean, I somehow couldn't find a way to get the patriarchy out of my bag and into the water. For two weeks, I clomped along with it haunting me like an aborted embryo. Meanwhile, *Ms.*'s financial problems only got worse. Our sister magazine *Sassy* was sold, the entire staff fired without warning. The *Sassy* editors' belongings were scattered throughout the office, the half-full water bottles and blinking computers evoking Pompeii. *Ms.* was assigning new articles while juggling several issues' worth of unpaid bills—and behind nearly every bill was a freelance writer or photographer or illustrator, virtually all women, who called each day wondering when her money was coming. We'd explain as well as we could the terrible position we were in. No one could say we were enjoying it; our life was hell and there was nothing to be done about it.

One day, Helen, the kind and mouselike Lang receptionist, called to tell me a writer was waiting in reception for me. I'll call the writer Wanda. Wanda had an annoying, vaguely British accent and stringy, *blah* hair. She had written a thousand-word arts piece for me about Marleen Gorris or Agnès Varda. I didn't particularly like the piece, or her, and she had already been much more aggressive about following up on her check than any of my other writers.

I geared up to explain to Wanda, yet again, that there was nothing I could do to expedite her payment and that I would let her know as soon as I knew anything. I steeled myself for anger, because I'd fielded a lot of it over the months of nonpayment. But when Wanda looked into my eyes, I saw something else: She was scared. "I am a single mother," she said, her eyes wet and her jaw tight, "and I need that money to pay for us to live. I need it right now; I've needed it for months. I am our only provider."

Wanda rattled me. Part of it was her literal desperation; part of it was knowing that she counted on *Ms.* to be responsible—to be a business, not an "ad-free magabook," or whatever it was I was so gleeful we'd become. The feminist ethos that made *Ms.* special meant I had to look Wanda in the eyes and, ideally, rectify the situation.

I don't recall exactly what happened next. I think I took her to the accounting department and requested an emergency check, but that might just be my delusions of heroism playing tricks on my memory. I do know that when I went home that night, I dug the plug of patriarchy wax out of my bag and flushed it unceremoniously down the toilet. A little after that, Lang sold *Ms.* to a guy who didn't want to pay the old debts, and soon after that, I quit.

I started working for places that weren't so pure, because I was now one of those freelance writers, unknown to the people in accounting, who needed to make a living. I pitched everywhere, and I felt naked without the label of *Ms.* editor to identify me. Gradually, however, I began to get offers and didn't need to be shrouded in the white wings of feminist publishing.

I had an idea I pitched to *Playboy,* about how women my age grew up with both that magazine and *Ms.* in their households, and how this reality normalized soft-core porn and feminism for my generation. An editor there, Bruce, liked it and called me into their

Fifth Avenue offices for a meeting. I was excited. I felt like a spy entering the headquarters of the patriarchy.

Bruce met me in reception. Vargas 1940s pin-ups prettified the already pretty walls, and a floating staircase bisected the grand space. Bruce was short—perhaps five-foot-six—with an unruly halo of blondish frizz. He complimented me on my outfit and my idea, and gave me the assignment to write a feature on contemporary feminism. The final piece featured interviews with Ani DiFranco, Guinevere Turner, Helen Gurley Brown, and Debbie Stoller. Bruce called me after I filed it. "I never say this," he said, "but I think this could win a National Magazine Award!" The article provoked huge debates at the editorial meeting: Half the staff thought it was bold and surprising, and the other half (which included the editor in chief) thought it wasn't right for *Playboy*. The latter half prevailed; Bruce was upset but made sure I was paid my full fee within the week of the story being killed.

I wrote pieces and tracked down my checks. I wrote a book with my former coven mate Amy Richards, then another, and then wrote two on my own. I got pregnant and had my son, Skuli.

As a single mother, I felt a newfound sympathy for the breadwinner. Not the Dale Langs of the world, whom I might still be able to write off as the devil, but the men and women who had to pay the mortgage, buy the diapers, and make sure there was food. Not paying that struggling Wanda still caused a pang of guilt, but I also felt a sense of solidarity with her. I was less and less pure, further away from the Emerald City of Feminism I thought I wanted and more focused on hunting down my checks. I requested higher fees partly out of self-esteem and partly because Skuli needed me to make more money. I hectored editors until I was paid. I had become Wanda. I no longer saw patriarchy as my nemesis or feminism's.

Like "the communist threat," the word "patriarchy" is at once unnecessarily shrill and too broad. The role patriarchy leaves for women—the child—is not just unappealing, it's inaccurate, partly because of the changes achieved by the Second Wave. In 1960, women couldn't have credit cards, make partner, fight in wars, or get pregnant at forty-five using a sperm donor. They *were* children in the eyes of the law, the culture, and themselves. Today, we have a male president who isn't traditionally masculine, and a first lady who is taller and older than her husband and was once his boss. We've had two presidents who were raised by single mothers and married women who were their equals, intellectually and professionally. Today, feminism's challenges are much more complex than good cop/bad cop—and that is true even while we deal with gender stereotypes that limit all of us and laws that erode women's freedom.

I have thought a lot about my father, who wasn't so stern, as it turns out. I once glibly characterized him as this stranger who came home at night tired and grouchy. Now, I add to that image one of him leaving for work each day before 7:00 AM in order to pay for college for his three daughters, or of the ulcers he got when we hit puberty and were sneaking boys into our rooms.

Just before I moved to New York, my father shaved off his mustache. I screamed when I saw his exposed upper lip for the first time. He seemed nude and vulnerable, like a turtle out of its shell. Was his threatening countenance no deeper than that handlebar of whiskers? It began to seem as if my father's scariness were merely a projection.

After the birth of my second son, my parents came to help. My father—still without a mustache—carried my days-old son around the apartment for hours, patting his back, rocking him, changing his diaper, and putting him down for naps. The word "patriarch" didn't come to mind while I watched him—but "father" did.

WOULD YOU PLEDGE YOUR VIRGINITY TO YOUR FATHER?

In a chandelier-lit ballroom overlooking the Rocky Mountains in the fall of 2006, some hundred couples feast on herb-crusted chicken and julienned vegetables. The men look dapper in tuxedos; their dates are resplendent in floor-length gowns, long white gloves, and tiaras framing twirly, ornate updos, the likes of which you often see in bridal parties. Seated at a table with four couples, I watch as the gray-haired man next to me reaches into his breast pocket, pulls out a small satin box, and flips it open to check out a gold ring he's about to place on the finger of the woman sitting to his right. Her eyes well up with tears as she is overcome by emotion.

The man's date? His twenty-five-year-old daughter. Welcome to Colorado Springs' Seventh Annual Father-Daughter Purity Ball, held at the five-star Broadmoor Hotel. The event's purpose is, in part, to celebrate dad-daughter bonding, but the main agenda is for fathers to vow to protect the girls' chastity until they marry and for the daughters to promise to stay pure. Pastor Randy Wilson, host of the event and cofounder of the ball, strides to the front of the room, takes the microphone, and asks the men, "Are you ready to *war* for your daughters' purity?"

Wilson's voice is jovial, yet his message is serious—and spreading like wildfire. Dozens of these lavish events are held every year; mainly in the South and Midwest, from Tucson to Peoria to New Orleans, sponsored by churches, nonprofit groups, and crisis pregnancy centers. The balls are all part of the evangelical Christian movement, and they embody one of its key doctrines: abstinence until marriage. Thousands of girls have taken purity vows at these events over the past nine years. While the abstinence movement itself is fairly mainstream—about 10 percent of teen boys and 16 percent of girls in the United States have signed virginity pledges at churches, rallies, or programs sponsored by groups such as True Love Waits—purity balls represent its more extreme edge. The young women who sign covenants at these parties tend to be devout, homeschooled, and sheltered from popular culture.

Randy Wilson's nineteen-year-old, Khrystian, is typical: She works at her church, spends most weekends at home with her family, and has never danced with a male other than her father or brother. Emily Smith, an eighteen-year-old I meet, says that even kissing is out for her. "I made a promise to myself when I was younger," she says, "to save my first kiss for my wedding day." A tenet of the abstinence movement is that having lovers before marriage often leads to divorce. In the Wilsons' community, young women hope to meet suitors at church, at college, or through family connections.

The majority of the girls here are, as purity ball guidelines suggest, "just old enough . . . [to] have begun menstruating." But a couple dozen fathers have also brought girls under ten. "This evening is more about spending time with her than her purity at this point," says one seven-year-old's dad, a trifle sheepishly. The event is seemingly innocent—not once do I hear "sex" or "virgin" cross anyone's lips. Still, every one of the girls here, even the seven-year-old, will sign that purity covenant.

Encouraging girls to avoid sleeping around is, without a doubt, a good thing. The same goes for dad-daughter bonding; research shows that girls who have solid relationships with their fathers are more likely to grow up to be confident, self-respecting, successful women and tend to make wise choices along the way. Question is, is putting girls' purity on a pedestal the way to achieve these all-important goals?

Fathers who are protective of their daughters' virginity are nothing new. "Keep your flower safe!" a good friend's dad used to tell her when we were in college, and we'd laugh—both because it was too late for her virginity and because there was something distasteful to us about his trying to control her sex life. Recently, though, protecting girls' virginity has become a national, not just familial, concern. In 1996, after lobbying by the religious right, Congress allocated nearly half a billion dollars for public schools nationwide to adopt sex ed programs that advocate abstinence only. Today, all but a few states use government money for classes that basically warn against any sexual activity outside of marriage.

The movement's latest mission is to make abstinence cool (it's been called "chastity chic"). There are Christian rock concerts where attendees sign pledges, sites like Geocities.com/thevirginclub that list stars who have held off on sex until marriage (Jessica Simpson, divorce notwithstanding, is one of their patron saints), and supportive bloggers (Abstinence.net features one called The Professional Virgin). Silver Ring Thing, a national abstinence group for teens, has an active MySpace page filled with comments like this from "Brianna": "I vowed to stay a virgin till marriage two years ago and it's been a long tough road . . . but it gets a lil' easier every day."

The first purity ball, with all its queen-for-a-day allure, was thrown in 1998 by Wilson, now forty-eight, and his wife, Lisa, forty-seven; the two run Generations of Light, a popular Christian ministry in Colorado Springs. "We wanted to set a standard of dignity and honor for the way the girls should be treated by the men in their lives," says Lisa, a warm, exuberant woman with a ready smile and seven children, ages four to twenty-two. Lisa's own father left her family when she was two, and despite a kind stepfather, she says, she grew up not feeling valued or understood. "Looking back, it's a miracle I remained pure," she says. "I believe if girls feel beautiful and cherished by their fathers, they don't go looking for love from random guys."

That first ball got some positive local and Christian press, as well as inquiries from people in twenty-one states interested in throwing their own. Today, South Dakota's Abstinence Clearinghouse—a major association of the purity movement—sends out about seven hundred "Purity Ball Planner" booklets a year (tips include printing out the vows on "beautiful paper" and serving wedding cake for dessert). While the Wilsons make no money from their ball, a cottage industry for accessories has sprung up. Roam the Internet, and you'll find a $250 14-karat pearl-and-diamond purity ring; for $15, you can buy a red baby-doll T-shirt with I'M WAITING emblazoned on the chest, its snug fit sending a bit of a mixed message.

The older girls at the Broadmoor tonight are themselves curvaceous and sexy in backless dresses and artful makeup; next to their fathers, some look disconcertingly like wives. In fact, in the parlance of the purity ball folks, one-on-one time with Dad is a "date," and the only sanctioned one a girl can have until she is "courted" by a man. The roles are clear: Dad is the only man in a girl's life until her husband arrives, a lifestyle straight out of biblical times. "In patriarchy, a father owns a girl's sexuality," notes psychologist and feminist author Carol Gilligan, PhD. "And like any other property, he guards it, protects it, even loves it."

When it's time for dads and daughters to take the pledge (some informally exchange rings as well), the men stand over their seated daughters and read aloud from parchment imprinted with the covenant: "I, [father's name], choose before God to cover my daughter as her authority and protection in the area of purity. . . . " The men inscribe their names, and their daughters sign as witnesses. Then everyone returns to their meals and an excited buzz fills the room.

Purity balls are, in fact, part of a larger trend throughout American culture of fathers spending more time with their daughters and sons—the amount rose from 2.6 hours a week in 1965 to 6.5 hours in 2000, the most recent year for which statistics are available. This togetherness has a real payoff for girls: Those who are close with their fathers generally do better in life than those who aren't. Dan Kindlon, PhD, a Harvard-based psychologist who did in-depth interviews with 113 girls and teens for his book *Alpha Girls,* found that those who had the best relationships with their dads were the most accomplished academically and had the strongest sense of self. Another much-cited study on the subject by two sociologists tracked 126 Baltimore girls from low-income families. It found that those with involved and caring dads were twice as likely to go to college or find a stable job after high school than those without such fathers; 75 percent less likely to give birth as teens; 80 percent less likely to ever be in jail; and half as likely to experience significant depression.

Of course, adolescence poses a tricky challenge: Teens are often more interested in hanging out with friends than in spending time with dear old Dad. And their fathers may not be sure how to treat a child who's morphing into a young woman. (I vividly recall the betrayed look my father gave me when he caught me, at fourteen, emerging from a make-out session in my room.) Some experts wonder if Dad's involvement in the family is seeming less important these days, given mothers' more dominant role—they're becoming the breadwinners in record numbers. Says Margo Maine, PhD, a clinical psychologist in West Harford, Connecticut, who often works with families, "Our culture—and even fathers themselves—underestimates the power fathers have on women's self-esteem and identity."

Randy Wilson wants to change that. With his bright smile, steady eye contact, and erect posture of a small but confident man, he reminds me of the magnetic self-help guru that Tom Cruise portrayed in *Magnolia*. "Way to go, men!" Wilson says. "I applaud your *courage* to look your daughter in the eye and tell her how beautiful she is. If you haven't done it yet, I'll give you a chance to do it right now."

I strike up a conversation with Christy Parcha, an eighteen-year-old brunette who's here to perform a ballet later on; her ten-year-old sister is attending the ball with their dad, Mike, a math teacher at a local community college. Christy's eyes are bright, her cheeks flushed, and a smile permanently animates her face. Although she just graduated from high school, she is not going to college but instead will be teaching ballet classes, continuing with piano lessons, and writing a book about "emotional purity," which Christy thinks is even more important than the physical kind. "I am just trying to reserve all those special feelings for my husband," she says ardently.

As it turns out, *not* allowing herself to think sexual thoughts makes her nervous, too, because she wants to experience pleasure with her future husband: "I don't want to be a burden to him in that I am not enjoying [sex]." Recently, a friend took her to see a movie about Queen Esther: *One Night with the King*—"a really romantic story," according to Christy. "So I watched it and I had these huge feelings rise up inside me, and I was like, 'OK, they are still there!'" she says, flopping back in her chair with relief. Still, Christy doesn't want to date. She associates sex outside of marriage as a girl "getting used, betrayed, having guys deceive you, all that kind of thing."

Other girls at the ball are far less eloquent about the pledge they've just made. To them, the excitement of the ball is buying fancy dresses and primping; one fourteen-year-old in the bathroom tells me she started getting ready at 9:00 AM. When I ask Hannah Smith, fifteen, what purity means to her, she answers, "I actually don't know." Her older sister Emily jumps in: "Purity, it means . . . I don't know how to explain it. It is important to us that we promise to ourselves and to our fathers and to God that we promise to stay pure until . . . It is hard to explain." I suspect that the girls' lack of vocabulary has to do with a universal truth of girlhood: You don't want to talk about sex with anyone older than eighteen, *particularly* your dad. At the same time, the girls seem so unsure of the reasons behind their vows that I can't help but wonder if they've just signed a contract whose terms they didn't fully understand.

There is no data on whether girls who attend purity balls remain abstinent until marriage; chances are, many do, given the tight-knit communities they live in. However, there is striking evidence that more than half of teens who take virginity pledges—at, say, rallies or events—go on to have sex within three years, according to findings of the National Longitudinal Study of Adolescent Health, the most comprehensive survey of teens ever taken. And 88 percent of the pledgers surveyed end up having sex before marriage. "No pledge can counter the fact that teenagers are, in fact, sexual beings post-puberty," notes Cary Backenger, a clinical psychotherapist in Appleton, Wisconsin, who works with teens, including several who have taken virginity pledges. "You can't turn that off."

Disturbingly, the adolescent health study also found that STD rates were significantly higher in communities with a high proportion of pledgers. "Pledgers are less likely than nonpledgers to use condoms, so if they do have sex it is less safe," says Peter Bearman, PhD, a Columbia University sociologist who helped design the study. For these teens, he believes, it's a mind game: If you have condoms, you were planning to have sex. If you don't, sex wasn't premeditated, which makes it more okay. The study also found that even pledgers who remained virgins were highly likely to have oral and anal sex—risky behavior given that most probably didn't use condoms to cut their risk.

Curiously, the teen pregnancy rate is on the decline nationwide. Proponents of an abstinence-only philosophy point to this as evidence that pledges work. But a study released in 2006 by the Mailman School of Public Health at Columbia University attributed 14 percent of this drop to teens' holding off on sex—and *86 percent* to teens' using more effective forms of birth control, like the Pill. Says study author John Santelli, MD, a specialist in adolescent medicine, "If most of the progress in reducing teen pregnancy rates is due to improved contraceptive use, national policy needs to catch up with those realities."

Leaders of the abstinence movement firmly believe, however, that teaching kids about the mechanics of sex and contraception "arouses" them, sparking them to have sex. They claim that those who break their vows were not "strong" pledgers to begin with, and that many more tend to keep them (teens the researchers didn't speak to). "Kids who abstain are not out there breaking hearts; they're not dogs in heat. They go on to have great, intimate sex," says Leslee Unruh, president of the Abstinence Clearinghouse. "The purity movement celebrates sex but not sex outside of commitment."

Girls who are getting married do need information about sex,

Unruh continues, and she's there to provide it. (On once occasion, "I had a girl call me from her wedding," she says.) "I let them know what to expect, that there might be some discomfort," and she gives detailed information about touching and lubricants when necessary. Unruh thinks purity balls are a commendable way to get girls who want to stay virgins to do so. As she says, "They help girls realize that their fathers care deeply about their future, and then they decide to keep themselves pure."

Many experts strongly disagree. "Virginity pledges set girls up for failure," contends Harvard's Dan Kindlon, who specializes in adolescent behavior: "I like the father-daughter bonding part of the balls, but it is unfortunate that it is around a pledge that is doomed. I always counsel parents to try to encourage teens to delay sex. But when you completely forbid teens to be sexual, it can do them more harm than good. It's like telling kids not to eat candy, and then they want it more."

"When you sign a pledge to your father to preserve your virginity, your sexuality is basically being taken away from you until you sign yet another contract, a marital one," says Eve Ensler, the writer and activist. "It makes you feel like you're the least important person in the whole equation. It makes you feel invisible."

It's not hard to imagine the anxiety young women must feel about being a purity failure. Carol-Maureen, an acquaintance from my hometown of Fargo, North Dakota, who got a purity ring in seventh grade and still wears it at twenty-two, told me, "If I had sex before marriage and my parents found out, I'd be mortified. I'd feel like I failed in this promise to them, even though it's really not their business."

Marie, a Texan I met through a colleague, took a virginity pledge at fourteen but actually felt no shame about breaking her vow a year later. "When I took the pledge, it was true in my heart.

But as I got older I had a broader worldview," she says. Still, as a teen she snuck around to have sex with her boyfriend so her parents wouldn't find out, and ended up getting pregnant at nineteen; she married quickly thereafter. Would she ever ask her son to take a virginity pledge? "*No,*" she says emphatically. "I don't want him to tell me something just because he thinks I want to hear it and then lie to me about it."

Figuring out your sexuality on your own terms is a major passage into adulthood. Back when I was nineteen and contemplating having sex for the first time, I presented my virginity to my boyfriend as this great treasure he could take from me. He looked at me and said, "But I don't want to take anything. You should be having sex with me because you want to—and if you don't, then you aren't ready." I was embarrassed by the smackdown of my "gift," but his words made me realize sex wasn't just something to give to him but something to do for myself, too. It required me to be active, not passive, lying there ready to be "taken." Learning that was more meaningful to me than actually having sex.

When I point out to Christy Parcha's father, Mike, that experience with relationships, bumps and all, can help young women mature emotionally and become ready for sex and marriage, he warily concedes that's true. "But there can be damage, too," he says. "I guess we'd rather err on the side of avoiding these things. The girl can learn after marriage." Like other fathers I speak with, Parcha says that if his daughter were to fail in her quest to be pure, she would be met with "grace and forgiveness."

But, he continues, "I am not worried about that. She is not even going to come close to those situations. She believes, and I do, too, that her husband will come through our family connections or through me before her heart even gets involved." Randy Wilson's oldest daughter, Lauren, twenty-two, met her fiancé,

Brett, a young man from the Air Force Academy, at church, and other fathers and daughters mention this to me as a hopeful sign that God will open similar doors for them. God has been throwing some curveballs lately, though: A week before the ball, Mike and Christy Parcha's pastor, Ted Haggard, a man who has openly railed against gay marriage, made headlines nationwide when he admitted to receiving a massage from a man (one who claimed Haggard had paid him for sex), showing how at odds what is preached and what is practiced can be.

Following dessert—chocolate cake or fruit coulis for the adults, ice cream sundaes for the girls—couples file into the adjacent ballroom. Seven ballerinas, including Christy Parcha, appear in white gowns with tulle skirts, carrying on their shoulders a large, rustic wooden cross that they lift up and rest on a stand. Lisa Wilson cries as she presents each of their three ceremonial dances, one of which is called "I'll Always Be Your Baby." Afterward, Randy Wilson and a fellow pastor, Steve Holt, stand at the cross with heavy rapiers raised and announce that they are prepared to "bear swords and war for the hearts of our daughters." The blades create an inverted "V" under which girls and fathers kneel and lay white roses that symbolize purity. Soon there is a heap of cream-colored buds wilting beneath the outstretched arms of the cross.

It's a memorable image at the end of a memorable night. I've been moved and charmed by the Wilsons, an uncommonly warm, polite, and loving brood. Over and over, the five daughters have told me how great their father is at giving them attention, love, and hugs. When Khrystian ballroom-dances with him, they look so comfortable in each other's arms that you wish *every* girl in the United States could have that closeness. But the real challenge, in my mind, is for a father to remain loving toward his daughter and at the same time nurture her autonomy. The purity movement is, in essence, about refusing to let girls grow up: Daddy's girls never have to be adults. "The balls are saying, *I want you to be eleven forever,*" says Dr. Kindlon. These are girls who may never find out what it means to make decisions without a man involved, to stand up for themselves, to *own* their sexuality.

I deeply wish that the lovely things I have seen tonight—the delighted young women, the caring, doting dads—might evolve into father-daughter events not tied to exhorting a promise from a girl that may hang over her head as she struggles to become a woman. When Lauren Wilson hit adolescence, her father gave her a purity ring and a charm necklace with a tiny lock and key. Randy Wilson took the key, which he will hand over to her husband on their wedding day. The image of a locked area behind which a girl stores all of her messy desires until one day a man comes along with the key haunts me.

By the end of the ball, as I watch fathers carrying out sleepy little girls with drooping tiaras and enveloping older girls with wraps, I want to take every one of those girls aside and whisper to them the real secret of womanhood: The key to any treasure you've got is held by one person—*you.*

—Originally published in *Glamour,* February 2007

Shelby Knox

I FIRST ENCOUNTERED SHELBY KNOX IN 2005 THE WAY
many people did: I watched the documentary about her battle for sex education in *The Education of Shelby Knox*. In the film, this plucky, outraged teenager from Lubbock, Texas, transformed from a conservative Christian purity pledger into an activist for sexual rights and sex education. At the time, Lubbock was a boomtown for teen pregnancy and STDs and was an ideal setting in which to document what abstinence-only sex ed had wrought. The Shelby of the film was sensitive and passionate—her face betraying every setback and lighting up with each new insight. By the end of the film, she was a feminist. I met Shelby in person in 2008 when she came to New York City to be a mentor at the Sadie Nash Leadership Project, a nonprofit that mentors young female leaders and activists. My frequent collaborator Amy Richards is a Sadie Nash board member, and she hooked Shelby up to house-sit at Gloria Steinem's apartment. Shelby ended up staying there for the next two years, soaking up and contributing to the feminist history in the making that is just part of Gloria's daily life. Over the years, her unruly

curls got shorter and her philosophies even deeper, but her outrage remained intact. A naturally charismatic and relatable speaker, Shelby now crisscrosses the country, advocating for comprehensive sex education and women's liberation, "Forth" Wave—style.

Jennifer: Who were you before *The Education of Shelby Knox?*

Shelby: I was a good Southern Baptist girl, raised in Mother Texas. I was a virgin and a good Republican. I took a virginity pledge when I was fifteen and had no inclination to question what was around me, because I was raised in a religion where it was a sin to question—and that extended to all parts of my life.

J: Now you're a queer-identified bisexual feminist! How did the filmmakers Marion Lipschutz and Rose Rosenblatt find you?

S: I had been working on sex ed in Lubbock for about six months, when I gave a horrible quote to the *Washington Post,* which said, "'There is nothing to do in Lubbock except have sex,' says 15-year-old virginity pledger Shelby Knox." The documentary people had funding to do a film on abstinence-only education, so they looked up Lubbock, Texas, found me, and started filming. They were mostly interested in my parents, who, despite being very conservative, were supportive of my work on sex education.

J: How did being followed by a film crew affect you?

S: Two things: It affected my activism, in the sense that I knew that we probably weren't going to succeed in Lubbock, but the film could provide a road map for other youth activists who were working on sex education. There was added pressure to get it right, to figure out the activism part so that other people could use the film. Second, I think it might have been much easier to dismiss a fifteen-year-old girl had she not had a New York City film crew behind her.

J: What did you think you were going to be when you grew up?

S: When I was really little, I thought I would be a professional Olympic gymnast. Then I thought I was going to be an opera singer. Then I thought I needed something more practical, so I was going to be a choir director. I was in that mode when the filmmakers showed up. The film came out in my second semester of college.

J: And how would you describe your career now?

S: I'm an itinerant feminist organizer.

J: What is an organizer to you?

S: An organizer is someone who puts in motion whatever the social action is that a community needs to effect change—whether it's petitions or getting people to a picket line.

J: And just what is a feminist?

S: Good question, Jen! I think the dictionary definition works, which is anyone who believes in the full economic, political, social, and cultural equality of men and women. I would add that a feminist also works toward that belief. I don't think you can just passively believe and be a feminist—you have to add action for it to have meaning.

J: Do you know people who self-identify as feminist but don't know how to actualize it?

S: I do, but I think not knowing how and being complacent are two different things and have to be addressed separately. For people who don't know how, plenty of blogs provide baby steps for becoming an activist.

For those who are complacent, I think that requires a personal trans-formation, discovering how their lives are impacted because of oppression and getting them to see their own lives as important enough for them to take action.

J: **You were born August 19, 1986, but I remember your saying that you thought you were Second Wave. Can you say more about that?**
S: I used to say that. A lot.

J: **Was it because you were living with a Second Waver?**
S: No, but Gloria had experiences that mirrored mine. She found feminism and felt like she saved herself—it was something completely new to her. I felt that way. I had never heard the word "feminism" growing up—not in a bad way, not in a good way; it just didn't exist. So when I discovered it, it validated my humanity and experiences and I understood it as the "world split open," which is the Second Wave phrase.

J: **Right. It was Muriel Rukeyser, the poet, who wrote "What would happen if one woman told the truth about her life? The world would split open." It's one of those great feminist mottos, like "the personal is political" or "a woman needs a man like a fish needs a bicycle."**
S: Now I identify as Fourth Wave, which I'm spelling a weird way in a book I'm working on—"F-o-r-t-h." I feel like we should put the motion back in the movement. You and Amy wrote in *Manifesta* that anyone born in the late '60s or early '70s grew up with "feminism in the water," and I think that is very true for your generation. The culture was still being directly impacted by the huge feminist changes of the '70s and even the early '80s. By contrast, my generation has two very different qualities: We are "backlash babies"—our moms thought if they didn't have it all, it was their own fault—and we are post-9/11. Have you read Susan Faludi's *The Terror Dream?* I think a lot of our cultural signifiers, our media, what we

have grown up with, are characterized by the regression of gender roles after 9/11. It's similar, but it's more of a *discovery* of feminism for my generation, rather than an *inheritance*. That impacts how one approaches both theory and action.

J: **Then can you reconcile for me the fact that transgenderism is way ahead of where it was when I was growing up and contextualize that liberation from gender roles within your argument about regression?**

S: The Third Wave has done everyone a wonderful service, especially in women's studies classes, by advancing theory about what gender means—unpacking that. Third Wave insists that activists approach everything with an intersectional lens. Intersectionality is our inheritance—perhaps more than feminism. When my generation begins to understand feminism, we understand it with the Third Wave interpretation that it must be intersectional. That is a given. I don't think feminism is necessarily a given—we have to discover it.

J: **What does "intersectional" mean to you?**

S: Each person has multiple identities, privileges, and oppressions, and they impact every part of one's existence; therefore, no activism or analysis can occur without taking into account those identities, privileges, and experiences. We still have to work on it—it's not automatic—but very few people come into feminism now believing that it is only about biological gender. They understand that it must have a racial analysis, a class analysis, discussions about what gender means, queerness . . . all of those things. It's not about analyzing men versus women or just men and women.

J: **So, you're saying that the Fourth Wave inherited complicated ideas about gender from the Third, as well as the idea that feminism must consider identities that intersect with and impact a person's gender. What are the contours of the Fourth Wave?**

S: First of all, we begin our activism online. Blogs are our consciousness-raising groups. There are a lot of Second and Third Wave feminists who say, "Well, they just blog and blog and they don't do anything else." In fact, blogs serve the purpose of helping us figure out our ideology, have disagreements with each other, and figure out what actions might work best without having to all be in the same place. They have equalized feminism, because you don't have to have the money to be in a women's studies class or be able-bodied enough to attend a consciousness-raising group every week or to stand on a picket line. I think one of the main contours of the Fourth Wave is that our activism is inseparable from technology.

J: **Kim France once wrote that the Second Wave's consciousness raising came in the form of big books such as *The Feminine Mystique* and *Sexual Politics*, but that the Third Wave's radical texts were songs by women like Liz Phair, L7, Queen Latifah, and Kathleen Hanna. The Fourth Wave's radical texts are Feministing and Racialicious?**

S: Yes. And we also do gender justice work through different venues than the traditional ones. My generation does work on reproductive rights, equal pay, and ending legal discrimination, but we also understand that gender justice lies in economic justice and justice for immigrants and queer people. My generation is saying that we as women have made ourselves a political interest group; politicians have started to feel like if they throw us a bone occasionally—like they don't ban abortion, or they provide a little money for the Violence Against Women Act—then they have done their part for women. My generation says, "Maybe we can be the more-than-half-the-population political force that we should be." We can ask, "How is this affecting women?" in every single room where politicians are making decisions.

J: It sounds like you are reasonably hopeful about your generation and feminism.

S: Are you finding people who aren't?

J: Well, I gravitate toward people who can see feminism in all of its vestiges, but I certainly know people who don't believe a Third Wave exists, much less a Fourth. That is, who don't believe that the younger generations have done much to progress or change feminism, just that we have lived amid its gains and taken them for granted. To people who say that there hasn't been any sort of contribution that is significant enough to be its own wave, what do you say?

S: To me, the Third Wave's significant contribution is the complicated analysis of feminism and gender. I think the Fourth Wave is still figuring out its contribution.

J: I think the Third Wave's major contribution is living the feminism imagined and put in place by an earlier generation. We manifested feminist theory.

S: The Third Wave was also instrumental in saying that feminism is not about women collectively. Although the movement aims to get what is best for most women most of the time, individual women's experiences matter. It broke down how individual women were living feminist lives. It wasn't a big mass of raging estrogen—

J: —all marching on Washington around that single issue we all agree is most vital!

S: Right. Third Wave pointed out that we are individual women with individual experiences. You said you didn't think your generation had a radicalizing moment. Do you think that the Anita Hill–Clarence Thomas hearings and the porn wars were that for the Third Wave?

J: There was a cluster of atrocities in the late '80s and early '90s, covered a lot in the media, to which the women who went on to become
Third Wave spokeswomen and Riot Grrrls were certainly reacting—
with rage. But I feel like it was more about finding one another—
taking gender studies classes or finding out that there were girls
who felt like you and they were creating zines and making music and
creating their own venues to express themselves. Those were radical
experiences. You say 9/11 and the Internet.

S: Yes, 9/11 and the Internet—and lately I have begun to think that Sarah
Palin is going to be big for my generation.

J: Well, she is already big to me, and I'm forty. I'm experiencing her as
a peer, and her very existence has had a big impact on my thinking
about feminism. She is embodying some stated goals of traditional
feminism—having more women in office, for instance, or having
women take the reins of power.

S: Yes, but it was Bella Abzug who said something like, "Women have the
right to start wars and be destructive and make bad policy decisions; I
support that right to my death, but I don't have to vote for them."

J: Other than that she often sounds not bright, not unlike George W.
Bush, what are Palin's anti-equality crimes? Part of what makes her
so riveting, I think, is that she is manifesting equality in some ways.
Her husband is more stay-at-home than she is; she has a career and a
pack of kids and a grandkid. . . .

S: She represents this media ideal of feminism—that isn't really feminist—
of being Wonder Woman, without ever discussing the mechanics behind
it, like the nannies. You can tell we are not even halfway there, because
that image really resonates with women. A lot of women believe that the
apex of success as a woman is to be able to "have it all." I think we have
learned that women can't have it all, usually because they have to do it

all and they don't have the support systems. If Sarah Palin were having it all and talking about the support systems she benefits from and figuring out ways to make sure that other women had those same supports, it would be valid.

J: So the antifeminist part of her—in addition to some of her stated political beliefs—is that she is allowing women to think that they can do what she does. That it just takes gumption. But, in fact, she has huge networks of paid support that she doesn't acknowledge. In effect, is she lying to women about how hard it is?

S: That is part of her antifeminist appeal. My generation has to work to undo the myths of the backlash, which said women had equality. Her co-option of Second Wave feminist ideology and language—completely perverting it—means that my generation must define what feminism is. It can't just be "everyone can be a feminist if you are female," as Palin says. We need a strict definition and ideology in order to go forward and to make change. Palin may incite us to define feminism faster than we otherwise might have.

—Interviewed on December 15, 2010

MY ILLEGITIMATE FAMILY

I got pregnant in early 2004, at the age of thirty-three. It was an accident, but the moment I saw that positive EPT, like *that,* I knew I'd have the baby. It felt right: exciting, grounding, momentous. The next day I told my best friend. "Wow," she said and then asked, "What did Gordon say?"

"I haven't told him yet," I replied. Gordon was my ex-boyfriend and the least compatible person I had ever met, much less dated. I'm an extroverted neat freak who counts Gloria Steinem as a role model; he's a misanthropic rock musician (and schoolteacher) with the social skills of Larry David and the hobbies of Homer Simpson. Our relationship reminded me of a *Sylvia* cartoon from the 1970s in which a feminist fairy tries to talk some sense into two love-struck opposites. "He's a member of the NRA!" the fairy yells. "And you have a bumper sticker that reads, I Brake for Hobbits!" Equally mismatched, Gordon and I spent a tumultuous year fighting and making up and annoying our loved ones with our drama, before we finally broke up.

While I had initiated the split in the midst of a flurry of actions designed to get my life in order, I found I couldn't quite make myself move on with anyone else. As the positive pregnancy test illustrated, a part of me was still involved with Gordon—the part that was enthralled by our chemistry, by his rakish handsomeness, by the effortless intimacy we felt, well, some of the time. That part of me was still sleeping with him, following once-a-week secret dates that camouflaged the daily conflicts that had led me to leave him.

I told him I was pregnant over the phone. And when he asked (with touching tenderness, I thought) if I was okay and whether I knew what I wanted to do, I said that I was going to have the baby. After all, I felt I could raise a child on my own, if it came to that. I met him hours later at a grocery store to pick up dinner, where he immediately grabbed me in a pythonlike embrace while Rod Stewart croaked, "Have I told you lately that I love you" over the tinny sound system. Gordon gazed into my eyes. "I wish this song wasn't playing," he said, and I laughed.

His response to the news was so right on that initially I thought we might be able to live together with the baby. But as my pregnancy progressed, our differences were once again painfully evident. I was tired, achy, nauseated—in other words, pregnant—and suddenly unable to meet for drinks and uninterested in going to 1:00 AM rock shows. Gordon, not pregnant, found he was repulsed by my frequent trips to the bathroom, constant milk shake drinking, and vomiting from the intense smells of summertime New York. In fact, Gordon seemed irritated about any extra help I needed and overly worried that having a child would make it harder for him to schedule band practice. He looked at dads pushing strollers and winced, as if fending off some future emasculation.

One August day, Gordon and I trudged to childbirth class during one of those New York City squalls where you are lifted up by gale-force winds and pummeled by rain balls. I was eight months pregnant. Once indoors, I began struggling in my manatee state to pull off my wet boots. The Alan Alda type on my left was waiting on his wife, making meaningful eye contact with her as if to say, *Thank you for offering your body to grow this child for us. I can never repay you, but I can subjugate myself to your mood swings and won't leave you because your breasts sag.* The suit-and-tie guy to my right jumped to assist when his wife grunted while attempting to remove her shoes. "Hey, could you give me a hand?" I whispered to Gordon, furtively eyeing Alan and Suit. Gordon sighed deeply, as if he'd had about enough of my Leona Helmsley ways, and said, "You want me to get down on my knees and remove your shoes?"

And that is when the truth dawned on me: I had manacled my life to someone who didn't want to be my partner. It was clear we couldn't live together, but I wondered if I was going to be able to be this baby's sole responsible parent and also shoulder the burden of dealing with Gordon, who acted like my other, not-so-cute child.

But shortly after this epiphany, something happened. Skuli was born, and Gordon fell in love—unselfishly and totally—with his son. We spent the first three months of Skuli's life in my tiny apartment. (Gordon still had his own place but wanted to live with the baby, and I was happy for the help.) But since we didn't need "together time," as we weren't romantically coupled, the second he got home from teaching in the afternoon, I could take off. Although the mother of a newborn, I still had time to take a walk, meet a friend, or go to a dinner party. Often, though, I would stick around and watch TV on the couch with Skuli while Gordon cooked dinner and took breaks to coo over our baby-acne-covered infant. When Skuli was about six months old, Gordon got a new apartment with a room for the baby, which he immediately filled with bizarre amounts of toys from FAO Schwarz. Skuli soon began staying over there at least two nights a week, which meant I even occasionally got to sleep in.

Because I wouldn't always be around, Gordon had to learn how to do all the stuff I did, when he might have not been the type to do so otherwise. And I was forced to give up control—something I wouldn't necessarily have had to do in a more traditional mother role. I couldn't micromanage Skuli's outfits, naptime, or food intake when Gordon was parenting, and so I learned not to. Thus, if Skuli showed up in red plaid shorts and an emerald green top, looking like a Christmas elf in July, I lived with it. I learned to trust that there was more than one way to take care of Skuli, and in that trust came the freedom for me to have a life.

Our wildly disparate natures even seemed to have purpose when it came to parenting. At my orderly house, Skuli has cleanliness, unbroken toys, and lots of friends and family coming over. At Gordon's creative house, they jump on the bed and toys never need to be put away, so you discover a bounty of old trains and robots under a couch pillow and—voilà!—new toys. (Gordon calls these found objects "play stations.") At my house, Skuli has a chalkboard; at his dad's, he is allowed to draw on his crib or on the floor. As a former city kid who was given a subway token at age twelve and told to "go play," Gordon takes Skuli to a museum or a zoo at least once a week. I bring Skuli to my childhood home in Fargo, North Dakota, where we sit on the lawn and listen to the mosquitoes.

Still, while I believe that this coparenting arrangement is best for everyone, Skuli might not agree. Around age three, after an Illegitimate Family dinner, Gordon was heading out the door, when Skuli said, "I don't want Daddy to go. He should stay." Gordon's face crumpled, and I felt like a witch.

As he got older, I heard this more, as we took on more of the contours of a traditional broken home. I feel a pang of loss that we can't all hang out in bed Saturday mornings and read the paper. I used to get weepy when I saw that Ford Freestyle commercial where the family has a fun day at the beach and then drops the dad off at his prefab divorce apartment. The tears well for a few reasons: the sadness of Skuli's having to say goodbye so often to one of his parents, but also the reassurance of knowing that there are so many once-together parents who now have joint custody (and manage just fine) that Ford is marketing to them.

Sure, sometimes I get furious because all my Tupperware has migrated from Skuli's lunch box to the black hole known as Gordon's kitchen, and I know to bring it up is to court a fight. But then I take a step back and I see my trajectory: from the EPT stick to the moment of clarity during childbirth class to the ritual end-of-night phone calls between Gordon and me to check in about Skuli. I really wouldn't trade any of it. We even have regular Illegitimate Family Night dinners to take the place of those old, secret dates. True, we are far away from the Jennifer and Gordon who were madly, chaotically in love, but the lasting benefit of that brief and ineluctable union is drawing on the walls right now.

—Originally published in *Real Simple* in March, 2008

Q&A

Björk: freaky momma

ONCE UPON A TIME, THERE LIVED A GIRL ON A BEAUTIFUL

isolated isle of extremes. She had two houses and two families, opposites themselves: The father's family was straight-laced, while the mother maintained a purple house full of hippies and radicals. The girl attended classical music school, recorded an album of Icelandic cover tunes in 1977 at the age of twelve, and became a punk/goth infidel as a teenager. Her band, the Sugarcubes, introduced her to fame outside of Iceland. At eighteen, she fell in love. She got married, got pregnant, wore a cropped shirt over her swollen belly, and sang "Like a Virgin" on Icelandic TV, reportedly provoking an old woman watching the tube to have a heart attack. She gave birth to a son, Sindri, at twenty. The marriage broke up. The band broke up. As a single mum, she moved to London with her son, and was true to her nature—independent. She *Debut*ed successfully in '93; after that came *Post*, a "Letter to Iceland." Which brings us to the present. Björk Gudmundsdottir, here in New York, sitting with me on the fire escape, sneezing like crazy because she's allergic to the cat that's roaming around here.

Jennifer: I read that a third of all births in Iceland are out of wedlock—but it doesn't seem to be stigmatized.

Björk: It's different, because family is so important. For me to have a baby at twenty and then be single, there is no problem because I was brought up in a massive family. Everyone just takes care of everyone. I think one reason why divorce is so common in Iceland is marriage is not taken so seriously. You love a person; if you don't love that person anymore, you don't live with them, because why suffer? All my ex-lovers, I haven't got tons or anything, but they're all mates of mine.

J: Are you concerned about raising Sindri in London, where he'll get messages that are sort of macho or sexist?

B: I think it's very important that he learns to judge for himself, you know? I was lucky enough to grow up in a society that is not so racist or sexist or all these things. Women in Iceland are quite independent. Women and men are equal. Unfortunately, they still go to jobs that are low paid— babysitting and all that—but we've got the most women in Parliament in the world, the head of Parliament is a woman, the president used to be a woman. The amount of women in high positions is the highest in the world. We've had to fight our feminist fights and all that bollocks, but it's like, "Mmm . . . so what?" It's no big deal.

You know, feminists really tire me, they really bore me to death. Especially my generation. I can relate to it if you're talking about my mother's age or my grandmothers' age and they're still angry and upset. I don't agree with everything she says—because we're human and we're different—but I have to agree with Courtney Love when she says she can't understand these feminists now. You've had a very aggressive feminist movement for over one hundred years! So for women to stand up and say [*in snotty American whine*], "It's just not the same, men get all the chances, it's so hard to be a woman today, rarara," they're basically dissing all the women in this century who have fought. They're saying there haven't been any fights fought, but there have been. You get women, like, twenty years older than me—they finally opened that cage. For women our age to say [*whine again*], "Oh, I'm in a cage, I wish I was born a man, and men suck, men are so macho—"

J: Wait, do you feel like women say that? Because I don't feel like I hear that so much . . .
B: Fffftttt. Oh, God, the arguments I get into at parties.

J: Really?
B: Oh, yeah! They're so bitter! The thing is, the cage has been opened and what you've got to do, a woman today, is walk out of it. I find with problems—you've got all sorts of different brands of problems—[sexism] is the kind where the more you talk about it, the bigger it gets, you see. Maybe, say, in America fifty years ago, it was necessary to talk and get the tumor and cut it open with a knife and get all dirty and ugly about it. Say, for example, being a single parent. A hundred years ago, being a single parent in the States, you couldn't financially—

J: And you would have been vilified—
B: Yeah, and all this morality *blahblahblah*. But today, there are no problems like that.

J: Well . . .
B: Well, there are. But you can make anything into a problem. If you're going to say, "Oh, I've got a baby, it's going to be so difficult," it is. If you work on it, you'll be fine. And I'm not just saying this in an arrogant way—"Oh,

that's all right of you to say because you've got money"—because I've only had money for, say, three years. I was a working-class, hardworking, single mother until then.

J: Did you feel like you were ready to have a baby when you had Sindri?

B: I was too young to even think about it. It just kinda happened, and I would do it completely different now. Not that I did it wrong or right, but I was twenty and I was like, "Oh, another person. Woohoo!"

J: What was the birth like?

B: I remember very stupid things, like the nurse kept giving me fruit juices instead of water and that really pissed me off. On the whole, it was one of my favorite experiences.

J: How has being a mother changed your creativity or your art?

B: It hasn't changed it at all, really. I can't really imagine it without it. You know, it's like saying, "If you had six toes, would you write different songs?"

J: Do you ever write specifically about motherhood or as if you were writing to Sindri?

B: No. I think motherhood is far more complex than that. If you get close to people, you keep swapping roles. You mother a person, and you mother yourself and you father yourself. You allow yourself to be an idiot and you do the same with your friends. And to say I'm only pro-tective towards my child, and when I meet my mother I'm really stu-pid, when I meet my boyfriend I'm really sexy, and when I meet my friends I'm really humorous—I think life is a bit more complex than that and you end up being everything at once. And that's kind of what I like about life—that you can't analyze it like that. You can't stand in front of your kid and say, "I'm your mother and you're my child." It's just not that simple, because you've got a friend for life in your child.

And sometimes, the kids, they protect you. I just find it quite funny that when you love someone—whether it's a child or boyfriend or whatever it is, a friend—it becomes so precious that you hide your ugly sides. Which I think is very funny, because when my friends show their ugly sides to me, I'm almost honored. That means you're very intimate with the person.

J: Do you think you're like your mother?
B: In some ways. I think I've got much more of my father in me. Both in the way I look but also my characteristics.

J: I've read in other interviews that you characterize your father as being very conservative and your mother as being a hippie.
B: That was probably more the two families than exactly them. They divorced when I was one, and my dad started a quite conservative family and a home that was full of people because he had another wife and, like, three kids. And my mom just invited all these friends to live with her, so I kept being the hippie amongst the conservatives or the conservative amongst the hippies. And I quite liked that; I was kinda the outsider always going, "Hmmm, but why can't we have one meal a day please?" and, "Why does everything have to be purple?"

J: You're still sort of an outsider—Icelandic culture is seen as so strange. . . .
B: I quite like that, you know? It seems to be my lot in life. I was at classical school and my grandparents only listened to jazz and I loved to go to my grandparents' house and play them Jimi Hendrix. Or go to the hippies and play them Simon and Garfunkel, which was pretty conservative to them. And then at school, doing the same thing. I could never belong to just one group. I would hang out with the disco fever people and play them punk tunes, hang out with the art-farties and kind of be the normal person,

and hang out with all the boys who did chemistry experiments and had insect collections and kinda be the—I don't know how to explain it.

J: Be the ambassador of all these different micro-cultures?

B: Yeah. I think I'm a much better Icelander abroad than I am in Iceland. In Iceland, everyone thinks I'm really foreign and eccentric and really strange and they don't understand me and my music sounds very awkward and foreign. And then I go abroad and they say, "Oh, you are so strange and awkward. That must be because you're from Iceland." I quite like that, you see. And then all the people I work with—say, one minute I'm working with a string quartet and the next minute I'm working with techno people and the next minute I'm working with the saxophone quartet and the next minute I'm working with a flute player—I always liked being the one being like, "Okay, that's cool, but have you thought about this?" and almost kind of gently say, "Listen, don't take this for granted. There's more to this." And not because I'm destructive, but just to kind of keep things alert. Alive.

J: How would you feel if your son was gay?

B: That was actually the first thing his father said when he saw him. Thor said, "It's a boy and he's gay." That's just his sense of humor. I laughed my head off and the doctors couldn't believe how insensitive he was. But that was exactly what I needed, just to have a laugh after all of that hard work. In a sense it would be quite handy because I wouldn't mind, instead of having a gay person being born into a family where they would make it into a nightmare for him. But you can't think that way—my son just has to be my son, doesn't he? I wouldn't mind at all, though. When we talk about boyfriends or girlfriends, we always talk about both possibilities.

J: For you?

B: For him. Or for whomever. 'Cause I've got a lot of gay friends and lesbian friends and they bring their lovers around and it's not taken for granted that it's the other sex. That's something that I think is sort of wonder-ful about this generation—I feel like my kids will grow up thinking that being gay is just normal, as opposed to being a tragedy.

J: What do you see as your mission as an artist?

B: I guess to smitten people. Meaning a lot of things; it depends on what day it is and what situation I'm in. I sing about emotion and sometimes it's sympathetic, sometimes it's to remind people of being alive. I'm not saying necessarily that I succeed all of the time, but that's my target, you see, that's why I'm still doing this job after all of these years.

J: How do you know when you're laying down a track, then, whether you've done that?

B: You can just feel it. I think people should not confuse it with something like "godly" or "otherworldly" or "supernatural" or "Ghostbusters" or "diva" or "power"—especially not power. It's the opposite. It's a very humble energy. It's kind of hard to describe without sounding really fake. It's just like when you meet someone the first time and you just know you're going to be great friends. It's like, how did you know that you fell in love or not? You just know.

J: Do you feel that music, or other kinds of art, has an obligation to innovate?

B: What I don't like about the word "art" is the fact that certain people are artists and certain people are not. The minute you think that this energy—like what you say, "innovative"—belongs to certain people and not to others, you've got it all wrong. Then you've got some sort of VIP or hierarchy of that energy. That energy belongs to everyone. You can be creative just by driving a taxi but you have a great sense of humor—I consider that very creative. I admire different people that can be in that kind of situation and still just come up with something that never existed before. At the end of the day, that's what creativity is about, coming up with something that never existed before.

J: Do you feel like there have been innovations in pop music in the past twenty years? Has there been a lot going on?

B: I'm just trying to draw attention away from the pop music thing and show that it's the same struggles that everyone is dealing with. So at the end of the day, you're born with ten fingers, two eyes, and a mouth and an imagination and you get, like, fifty or sixty years out of life. It's your duty to use what you've got and not just put yourself to sleep or function like a robot. It doesn't matter what job you do; to wake up in the morning and actually find that day exciting is the biggest victory you can do. And then, say, to do a song like that, which is my job, sing them and go [*intake of breath*] just before I go onstage, I'm like, "Woohoo!" It's just an appetite for life and enthusiasm; life wins death—one-nil. And I'm always trying not to be philosophical or deep but, for me, it's everywhere. It's not just in pop music.

J: I was wondering if you could describe your life in terms of a fairytale.

B: Well, I think it is a fairytale. I find it very tiring when people think magic is like in David Copperfield or like in *Ghostbusters*. No, I totally, just to set the record straight, I believe, I'm very much into magic and fairies. Yeah. I'm probably the biggest fan of magic realism there is. You know, Lorca, Frida Kahlo. The sagas of Iceland are similar to that: down-to-earth, commonsense, bread-and-butter. It is real. And I don't believe in escapism, fantasy, I believe in the magic that is just there. But I can't, say, write out of my life because that would kill it. I don't want to know what happens next, you know? That's very important to me.

—Originally published in *Bust* magazine, Fall/Winter 1996

HOW TO DO
EVERYTHING WRONG

CONCEPTION: After psychologically disturbing visit to childhood home, solo, for holidays, have crazy, drunken breakup sex with ex-boyfriend. Don't use birth control.

PREGNANCY: Be freelance and have the kind of "catastrophic" insurance that covers something if you are hospitalized, but not sonograms, medicine, or doctor visits. Have no end of small problems for which you have to see the doctor, including thinking you are leaking amniotic fluid in seventh month. (Turns out it's urine, which is at first a relief and then disturbing in its own way.) Spend a week believing you have gestational diabetes, but later it's discovered that it was the glass of Mountain Dew you drank just before the blood test.

BIRTH CLASS: Attend with ex, who openly resents any homework and bolts before class is over each week to get a drink at neighborhood bar. Wonder if it would be more or less embarrassing to go alone.

LABOR: Wake up feeling crampy and dig out yellow Wonderbra you've never worn before; don it. Go to hospital five hours later and immediately beg for an epidural. Get an epidural that pools so that your left hip is numb but everything else is in full bloom of pain. Make mental note that you don't have pain relief, nor will you get credit for having a natural birth. Say to anyone near you, at first abashedly but with increasing volume and abandon, that you "really feel like" you have to "poop." Although all other clothing has been removed, keep yellow Wonderbra on for entire labor and delivery.

BIRTH PARTNER: Ex is there but leaves during transition to make phone calls. When he comes back, he takes one look at your vagina and blanches. Ex attempts to comfort you through contractions by making out with you; stands on IV.

DELIVERY: Scream bloodcurdling scream until son finally comes out. Baby is immediately whisked to neonatal intensive care unit. Head to hospital room and become the only person on the floor without a baby. Feel foolish.

BONDING, PHASE 1: Visit child in NICU but feel like interloper. Ask timidly if you are "allowed to breastfeed." When son finally comes home (day four), experience feeding child as akin to placing a snapping turtle on your swollen, chapped nipples. Notice son has little pimples and have flashback to terrible high school years when you had zits.

BONDING, PHASE 2: Son is now covered in white and red pustules and looks not unlike Elliott Smith. When people come to see him, blurt out, "Can you believe how bad he's got baby acne?!" so that they know you know it's there. Feel bad that this is the first thing you say about your child. Try to pump bottles so Baby Daddy can do 4:00 AM feedings, but "allow" the occasional bottle of formula (okay, use formula every night).

COPARENTING: Swing between smugness that you and baby's father literally share the work and expense of child rearing, unlike most "real" couples you know, and blind rage that you have to parent with irrational man you broke up with two years ago. Wag finger in ex's face and whisper sotto voce threats that you won't follow through on.

BEDTIME: As child grows older, have him on late schedule so he'll sleep in the morning. By the time he is twelve months, his bedtime is 10:00 PM; by eighteen months, it's midnight. Keep this a secret from friends, relatives, and your own parents.

SCHOOL: Take son to preschool the day after he turns two. Sneak out of school, sniffling, when he isn't looking because that's your strategy when you leave him with baby sitters. Walk home talking on cell phone to sister about how son is in school and next thing you know you'll be taking him to college, when other line beeps in. Learn that son is hysterically crying—"desperate," as the teacher terms it—and that you are to pick him up immediately. At the pickup, start to cry when teacher asks if you even said goodbye to son before leaving.

PSYCHE: Notice son winds his tresses in his fingers as he is falling asleep, plucking out many strands during each nap, creating small bald spot.

FOOD: Son appears to consume about a gallon of milk every day, eggs, and very little else. He asks for Tic Tacs and cough drops as a treat, demanding in a loud, rude voice, "Need Tic Tac! Need Tic Tac!" Try to resist giving child Tic Tacs or cough drops, as it seems weird and he's crunching them and probably going to break one of his tiny teeth. Despite anorexic's diet, son is extremely tall. Sometimes he will emerge from his bedroom chewing on something and when you inquire what, he'll say, "Hair."

PSYCHE, PART 2: Notice son gets up from a nap covered in strands of hair. Call pediatrician for advice. Pediatrician says to ignore that son is pulling out hair ritualistically, that son is soothing himself, like thumb sucking. Ignore hair pulling for one day and then take to whispering intensely to son not to pull his hair; you'll give him cough drops if he'll stop pulling hair. *Please stop pulling hair.*

LOVE: At son's school, three weeks into the term, as you are fluffing his hair to obscure thinning areas, receive wet, mentholated kiss from balding two-year-old. Wince as heart nearly breaks from how lucky you are.

—Originally published in *Babble,* December 2006

ALL THE SINGLE LADIES

The summer of 2007, when my son Skuli was almost three, I flew back early from a trip to Fargo so I could attend a party for Jenny and Sara Jane, two friends of mine who were celebrating their five-year relationship. Jenny and Sara Jane were a decade younger than I, Smith graduates with great style and even more beautiful politics. I was excited to go to their ceremony, which struck me as risky and brave. Their families weren't always comfortable and on board with their daughter's sexuality. Having everyone convene for this celebration of a gay relationship was, to my mind, a big deal. I was hungry for examples of alternative family-making, having logged nearly three years as a single mom by choice.

I was used to traveling alone, but that didn't make it any more pleasant when things went awry. Skuli was easy, but it wasn't like I had another adult to carry the bags, figure out the missed connection, or help clean up the milk vomit after the bumpy flight—things which happened with annoying regularity. It was a blazing hot July afternoon when we arrived at JFK after a long flight. I threw our bags in Skuli's Sit 'n' Stroll, a car seat/stroller combo that I used in airports like a wheelbarrow when I traveled with him. Carrying him on one hip, I slogged out to the long-term parking lot. Our car, a 17-year-old red Honda Civic, shimmered in the heat. *This isn't good,* I thought, heart sinking, because one of the many quirks of this vehicle (passed down from mother to sister to me) was that it wouldn't start when parked in direct sunlight. I fastened Skuli's car seat into the cauldron of the backseat and turned the ignition, praying it would turn over. Nothing. I waited two minutes. Still nothing. Again—

"We should call someone to help us," Skuli offered from his microwave oven perch. He was good at intuiting our next step.

I called someone (JFK Roadside Assistance, maybe?) and soon a young guy arrived to jump our battery. "It's not the battery," I said, wishing I had thought to pack snacks and a water bottle for Skuli. "This car doesn't start in heat. I have to wait until sundown."

"It's the battery, Ma'am," the car guy said. After ten more minutes of needless jumping, hope, and disappointment, he offered to drive us in his tow truck to the nearest garage. Feeling a familiar financial panic, I mentally calculated the cost of this crisis—$60 for tow, $50 for car service home, God knows how much to "fix" the car (i.e., let car come to room temperature)—and wondered if witnessing Jenny and Sara Jane's commitment was worth the expense. I decided it was. We got home in time for me to shower and change, drop Skuli at his dad's for the night, and head to the party.

On a Brooklyn rooftop that night, drinking restoratively, I met Sara Jane's mom. A former nurse with great bone structure, frosted blonde hair, and a mini dress, her whole body vibed, "Be surprised that I have two adult daughters." She was a former single mother, and as we continued to drink and listen to the iPod playlist Jenny and Sara Jane had selected for this night, she prodded me for stories about my life. After each story, she'd shake her head and say, "Be selfish, Jen. You've *got* to be selfish."

I was used to getting unsolicited advice about my life, especially from people I considered to be less than knowledgeable. Some of it I gratefully accepted, like the offers to come over for Sunday dinner, and the used baby equipment my friends were always finding for me. Sometimes, though, I sensed not so much helpfulness but pity. I mean, I felt bad for some of *them*, what with their unhappy marriages and wilting sex lives, but I got the feeling that they used me to feel better about their own lives. "I know it must be so hard," these friends would say, flattening me into a stereotype with their sympathy faces (furrowed brow, lips pressed into a droopy frown) and their "Does Skuli have male role models? Is his dad, you know, *involved?*" concerns.

The truth is, it *was* hard. I woke up in the middle of the night worried about bills, anxious that I'd have coverage for Skuli while I was working. I brought him to parties with me not because he loved hanging out at adult's houses at 11:30 PM, but because it was that or never socialize. But . . . I was *happy*. I'd never felt so much love and independence at once.

Back at the party, I attempted to respond to Sara Jane's mom. As a single mother, I was not self*ish*—that suffix "ish" connoting something gross or halfway. It's more like I was self-full. It was definitely a time in my life in which I had to rely on myself more than ever before, and yet my life was very rich with other people: Christine dropping by on the way home from work because I've conveyed that friends are always welcome, saying yes to spontaneous invitations to the Bronx Zoo because Skuli and I don't have to negotiate anyone else's schedule, New Year's Eves with Amy and Peter, sleepovers at Gillian's because we only need one bed.

The nuclear family, I noted, was a more *closed* home, electrons orbiting around the nucleus of the dinner table, ordered primarily by the schedules of its members. In my single-lady status, my home was open. I controlled the doors and I wanted people to come in. My friends and family showed up for me all of the time. My sister Jessica, happily married and also a mother, marveled at how much help from friends and family I marshaled. "I guess I'm not afraid to ask," I said, attempting to analyze the discrepancy. "And people assume I need it, of course, which is kind of humiliating."

"Not as humiliating as needing it even though you have a partner," Jessica responded.

Clearly, Jessica wasn't one of the condescending types, but I gravitated toward single parent friends after Skuli was born. We were the ones who always dropped our kids late at school and got stern, condescending looks from the teachers. We brought our children to cocktail parties and readings, because it was that or we couldn't go. The single moms had scuffed shoes; our roots grown out from a little too much time between hair appointments. Superficially, we were more bedraggled, but we were also a really sturdy, actualized crew. Alan (as a man, an honorary single mom) was a poet, professor, and art critic who kept a perfect house for himself and Sophie. Sixty-something Merle owned the largest abortion clinic in the country and became a self-made millionaire before adopting Sasha from Siberia. Liliana had left Poland, escaped her abusive husband, and was raising Anna and Alex while working full time and going back to school. Sally wanted the baby but not the bad-boy baby daddy, and was raising her son exactly how she wanted—with organic food, no sugar, and lots of travel. Lorraine had three children, two exes, three enormously successful salons, and, in spite of being dyslexic, had written a book. We shared a common currency—the bracing combination of independence and terror. The independence was precious—"I get to write three nights a week," as Alan would often say—but it was the terror (food on table! clothes on kid! Insurance! Tuition!) that kept us motivated.

I felt lonely some days—the obvious ones, like Valentine's Day and Mother's Day—but the other days I felt this magical self-reliance. "Trust thyself," as Emerson wrote, "every heart vibrates to that iron string." I had ample opportunity to learn to trust myself, and maybe opportunity (also known as necessity) is just what one needs. Single parenthood was good for me, but people tend to feel bad for the children of single mothers, too, I noted. The assumption was that boys needed a role model and girls needed to know their dad would love and protect them. Heading into the subway one day, I was struggling with the stroller (Skuli in it and heavy) and my bags. Out of the corner of my eye, I saw a teen thug walking toward me with a menacingly blank look on his face and his pants drooped. He leaned over, picked up my carriage and, without a word, carried Skuli down the two flights of stairs to the subway platform. I sputtered a thank you. He looked me in the eye and said in a soft voice, "I was raised by a single mom, Ma'am."

My friend Amy was raised by a single mom. When she turned thirty, her friends made a book for her, each of us taking a page to extol her work ethic, dance ability, and generosity. Her mother's page had a snapshot of the two of them, taken when Amy was about five and her mother was in her young twenties. The photographer was behind the two. Her mother is pointing at a flower right in front of them, showing it to Amy. And Amy is pointing up and away, to something that her mom can't even see. She wrote that it wasn't the most flattering photo of the two of them, but it was a good example of their relationship. The caption Amy's mother wrote was "We make a good team. We make a good team."

The fact that she wrote it twice slayed me, but I was most struck by seeing my tough, confident, sunny friend cry as she read the words. I think Amy knew that thing that I know and that Skuli knows and that all of the single moms know: the joy, beauty, and hard-earned satisfaction of being a good team. Days before that awful moment at JFK when my car wouldn't start, we visited my cousins at their lake cabin in Minnesota. Their house was crawling with kids and my cousin and her husband appeared to have an attractive, invitingly healthy relationship. The kids swam and hunted for minnows and played with toy cars. When it was time to leave, Skuli threw himself on the ground and cried, "No, I won't go! I *belong* here."

He had done the same thing a few weeks earlier at Amy's house, at which there was the same appealing constellation of happy and fun parents, cool toys, and siblings. Both times, I felt a chill course through me, because his response struck me as maybe true and certainly insightful. Not that he needed to have two parents, but there was something about the joviality and regularity of that home that either vibrated with what he knew about other people and missed in his own life—or it just felt right in some meaningful way that his three-year-old self needed to assert.

To me, it hurt, because I knew I belonged with him but I didn't belong there—and I wanted him to believe, as I did, that we were lucky that things had worked out as they did, that our lives were unique and wonderful. Was I just being selfish?

"Be selfish"—these words echoed in my brain the summer Skuli was three. What did it mean? Was it selfish to stay a unit of two, because Skuli would have to shoulder the burdens of my aging alone? Or was it selfish to have a love life when I had a young child who needed me? I could see it both ways and many more.

It may have just been a coincidence, but after that "selfish" conversation, I got my mojo back. By mojo, I mean my sexual self. I began dating again later that month, and within a few weeks I met the man that would become the father of my second child and, later, this same man—BD—became my husband. Skuli has thrived in our nuclear family, stricter and more constant than what he knew before. I wonder sometimes if he remembers our former way of being. Will he know to help a struggling mom with her stroller in ten years?

"We don't spend as much time together," Skuli told me one day, while walking home from school. We were holding hands and he had been telling me about his life in an alternate universe he calls Boneland. "You spend a lot of time with BD now."

I squeezed his hand.

"Remember when we were just the two of us," Skuli asked, "and we'd sleep together in the same bed?"

"I do remember," I said. "We made a good team, Skuli."

We made a good team.

Q&A

Ani DiFranco

THERE WAS A TIME IN THE MID-'90S WHEN I BEGAN

to feel the core of my generation assert itself. I worked at *Ms.* magazine at the time and was frequently asked what my peers had done for
feminism lately. Liz Phair and Courtney Love were being hailed as feminist
thinkers in *New York* magazine, Rebecca Walker was coining "Third Wave,"
and *Bust, Bitch,* and *HUES* were saying you could be a feminist and care
about pop culture. During that time, I looked to Ani DiFranco (my exact
same age) as a beacon, inspiring me to believe in the daughters and sons
raised in the wake of the Second Wave. First, there was her example of
independence: She wrote her own music, played her own guitar, had her
own label, Righteous Babe, owned her publishing . . . the list went on. But
most of all, there were her poetical, philosophical lyrics, which always
seemed to comment directly on my own innermost thoughts. It was as
if Carol Gilligan and Shulamith Firestone had made a baby with Sappho.
Or Dorothy Allison had mated with Flo Kennedy. Ani wrote revenge fantasies about bleeding through one's pants in public, love songs to men and

women, breakup songs to men and women, goodbye songs to fetuses, and beautiful odes to voting.

At *Ms.* I was often asked who the new feminist leaders were. "Where is your movement?" they'd wonder. I'd point to Ani and then paraphrase a lyric of hers I especially loved: "Every time she moves, she makes a women's movement."

Jennifer: I was hoping we could talk a little bit more about being a mother and how that's informed your thinking about feminism. It's made me think about misogyny. I don't think my sons hate me yet, but I feel like the process of their growing independent involves some betrayals on my part—just saying no or helping them do things on their own, even when they don't want to—and they betray me sometimes by not needing me. That's the process of differentiating and growing up, but how might this profound relationship and dependence between a baby and its mother contribute to misogyny? For both to survive—psychically and physically—they have to learn to be separate.

Ani: The whole process of birthing and then mothering, nurturing, growing the next generation is a real potent reminder of the basis of feminist thought. Feminism springs inherently out of this experience that is unique to women. The male child especially has to separate to become himself. Not only the creature realizing, *Oh, I'm not my mom*—as they're sucking on a big tit—*I'm separate;* the male child has to go much further with that separation in order to realize himself than does the female child. I haven't been wondering so much about the journey from there to misogyny, as I've been thinking about the female journey and how this very early experience of connectedness, of oneness with the mother that then is continuous through the whole life, is a very useful experience in terms of saving humankind from doom.

Yes, we are autonomous, in a sense. Yes, we are individuals, in a sense. But an even more important truth in the twenty-first century is, we are *not* autonomous; we are connected. We only exist in relation to each other, and we couldn't exist without each other. That focus on relationship and the connectedness is inherent to female development, and therefore female thinking, and it is that sensibility that is lacking in our big social and political structures.

J: It's *In a Different Voice.*

A: Yes. I long for the whole world to read that Carol Gilligan book, because it changed my life. Gilligan identifies the squashing and marginalizing and otherwise ignoring of the female understanding that comes out of female experience. We deny our connections to one another, and this is at the root of many of our social problems. We think we can make nuclear waste and then dump it over here, where we can't see it; then that's okay.

When you have a baby, there is no more question as to whether you are separate. The baby body comes out of your body and remains connected to your body for a long time. Any mother puts that relationship, and the needs of her child, before anything else. The role of mother on this planet has some very, very deep wisdom. Taking part in that has really reblossomed my feminist understanding.

J: There was another chapter in *In a Different Voice* that was about women post-*Roe* and how they were grappling with power. They characterized their reproductive decisions, once they had the power, as "selfish," whether or not they were continuing the pregnancy or having an abortion. Gilligan noted that putting self first is—or at least was—really difficult for women.

A: I feel that women have grappled with that since the dawn of time. I imagine that most of the backlash towards women gaining power in society was not the fear women had of their own power, but the fear men had of women's power.

J: **You wrote the introduction for the natural-childbirth leader Ina May Gaskin's latest book, *Birth Matters*. The central premise of her book is that giving birth is an incredibly powerful experience, and that when women fully engage with that experience, that power and confidence will help them for the rest of their lives, essentially. I can imagine birth is a core experience of empowerment. At the same time, I've seen a lot of my friends profoundly disappointed when they ended up having a C-section and feel like they didn't even give birth.**

A: I know. It's tragic. It's very hard to speak on, because there are so many women out there, all around us in our society, who have been denied that experience. I have done very little talking onstage about my own child's birth, because the potential to make women feel bad is so much greater than the potential for teaching and sharing and growing together. I'm surrounded by educated feminist women who have all had C-sections. There are, of course, many different levels of intervention, and not one thing is right for everybody, certainly, and women should be free to have choices.

I don't think you need to give birth naturally to be a fully empowered or realized woman—there is more than one way to skin a cat—but in terms of the whole of womanhood, we cannot do without it. When you disrupt the flow of natural childbirth on a mass scale, you cut off one of humanity's essential connections to creation and you dampen the overall level of consciousness.

J: **Describe your experience.**

A: The experience of childbirth, for me, ironically, was humbling instead of empowering. That lesson in itself is so important. You really feel small. You feel helpless. You feel insignificant, because you are. It's such a colossal, physical event. It's bloody, it's violent. Nature is unconcerned with your individual survival. Those are important blows to the almighty ego.

I seem very strong and willful on stage, but in the one-on-one, I'm not that way, and I knew that for me, if I went into a hospital, I would have had at least an epidural, and I probably would have had a C-section because they certainly wouldn't have tolerated three days of labor. I definitely would have been a statistic, just by going into that environment. The only thing I knew to do for myself was to stay away. Beyond that, I had no idea.

I read all my Ina May and I was gunning for an orgasmic birth. *This is going to be beautiful! I am going to have rushes and it's going to be powerful and I'm going to feel one with all mothers and I'm going to smile as she comes out!* Of course, it just kicked my ass. I was terrified. I was alone. It was the most awful thing ever, but the fact that I went through the most awful thing ever and came out on the other side . . . I have that in my pocket. That's the female experience that, when it's denied on a mass level—of course, you must allow for emergencies— but on a mass level, the denying of the female experience is going to be a denial of female psychology.

Speaking on birth in a culture like this is very tricky, because the last thing women need is more people telling them that they fucked up and they were weak or something. The whole point is that we're not weak.

J: **Can you talk about growing older and the self-critical voice with which many women and girls are very familiar? You write about it in your song "Present/Infant."**

A: I've had that voice my whole life, although it's sort of getting quieter now that I'm older, because I just throw a blanket over it. I learned it from society and I learned it from my mother, who hated the way she looked.

She just didn't stack up well in a society where a female's face is her currency and it's all very explicit what is a valuable female and what is a not-so-valuable female. My mother was somewhat crushed by that, and she taught me to be, too.

J: So you grew up seeing your mom look in the mirror and not like how she looked?

A: No. None of it was spoken. It was all learned without words. There were no mirrors in my house growing up. There still are no mirrors in my mother's house. I learned that pretty women are the best women and I'm not one of them, without any words spoken whatsoever.

J: What do you think your daughter is learning from you?

A: My daughter, Petah, is a little bit of a tomboy. She's four, but she's not about princesses at all, whereas most of her little female friends are. She's into purple, not pink. I am very conscious, when people give me books or things for her that are of the culture that female beauty is female worth. I give them away. I ache for her to not learn certain things about this world, the social heirarchy. There's that. There's also the race thing. Another thing I'm very conscious of is to not label people in front of my daughter—black, white, this, that, the other—because she doesn't label people that way. She talks about people's gender incessantly, but never their color.

J: How does Petah understand gender?

A: At about the age of three, she became transfixed by gender. She went through her whole class at preschool: "Piper is a girl, Christian is a boy, Josephine is both." I'd be like, *Whoa, really?* Josephine is her classmate, another three-year-old. One of her two female teachers, she designates as both. My friend Animal, who is a female but very much a tranny, she designates as a boy. So her understanding of gender is that it's very important, that it's a fundamental part of your nature, and that the distinctions between the two sexes are important but also very fluid.

I say, "Don't you think Animal's both?"

"Hmm. No. Animal's a boy."

Wow, cool. Her grandmother, my mother, she designates as both, and I agree.

J: Can you tell me how you define feminism when you're forced to define it?

A: My personal idea of feminism is more complex than rights and opportunities. That's the social meaning of overcoming patriarchy, but the purpose and the importance of feminism are bigger than liberating women. Feminism is a philosophy that favors interdependence and cooperation over hierarchy and competition. It's the feminine sensibility, based in the maternal experience, of prioritizing relationships and other people over individual pursuits and self. And it's the social movement against patriarchy and towards balance between the masculine and the feminine in all aspects of human society.

J: That's good! I'm learning so much about what feminism can be by asking others to define it. How has marriage affected you as a feminist?

A: My marriage has, in many senses, saved me, because it's a marriage based on true, true love and mutual respect. Before I met this man that I now call my husband, I had terrible TMJ. My jaw would snap every time I bit a cracker. I had a very poor immune system. This was my idea of myself, that I get sick all the time; if anybody is sick anywhere, I will get it. I couldn't sleep. I'm an insomniac. All these things I *knew* about myself changed after he started loving me. It took years for my jaw to loosen, for my immune system to start working again. Basically, his love has made me happier and more relaxed than I've ever been, more okay in my skin, more okay in my life, just the way his love holds me up.

That's the beautiful thing marriage, love, respect, and security can do for somebody and have totally done for me.

J: Any negatives?

A: Well, I do all the dishes! I clean the house. My mother was an early feminist. She was outraged to be doing all the housework, taking care of the children, and cooking when she got home from work. I inherited her outrage, and that righteous anger has been a part of my art and my growth. Coming back around to standing at the sink, doing dishes *without* outrage, has been a long journey for me.

In the beginning, I was like, "I'm doing dishes? But I should be writing a song! What are you doing? You're on eBay! You should be doing dishes while I write a great song." Then I realized that great songs are not the only things the world needs. The world needs food. The world needs love. The world needs clean dishes. The fact that I actually have to dedicate my time to these humbling caretaking activities that women do is good for me and good for my soul. It's been a really interesting, circular journey. I'm part of the amount of care that women put out in this world. I labor to keep my self-respect and keep an understanding that this is important.

J: You are an artist and a big success, a breadwinner, so I'm assuming you don't feel reduced to domestic activity. The issue with the domestic sphere, or at least it was for my mom, was, she felt her effort wasn't really seen. She cleaned and cooked and created the home, and at the end of the day, we'd just mess it up.

A: Yes, and that's the problem with patriarchy. Women can become reduced to caregivers, and giving care is not honored. When women do that daily service, daily caregiving, it's not seen or respected in the way that running a Fortune 500 company is. The problem is with the society that doesn't honor, value, or listen to it, not with the female role in itself. The problem is with the society that does not care for the caregivers and insure their freedom.

J: **I'm married too, and I feel it's been interesting, not from him but from others, how much my sexuality is questioned: "So, you're straight?" It has been gratifying to have my sexuality continuously directed toward my husband, this person whom I love and helped create my family. The fear I struggle with is having profound relationships in my past blotted out.**

A: "I always knew you were straight" is coming from a place of "you were pretending" and "you're a faker." All of that defensive "us" and "them" thinking comes from an unsafe society, where you need to know who is on your side and who's not because that could be life or death when you walk out on the street. If we had a society that understood sexual fluidity and was not afraid of people changing as they grow up and older, then we would be able to freely talk about our experiences and our own changing nature. When I married my first husband, I heard, "Fraud! Sham!"

J: **By this marriage, you just must be so over that critique.**

A: I say to "straight girl!" the same thing I say to "dyke!": "Whatever."

—Interviewed on March 18, 2011

BREAST FRIENDS

When my son was a few months old and my dear, dear friend Anastasia was at the end of her pregnancy, she turned to me one day and said, "I have a request."

"Anything," I said. After all, she had come over two or three times a week since my baby was born to help me as I finished writing a book. She'd done everything from returning phone calls to burping the baby to vacuuming. When she tipped over in the course of trying to rock my son, Skuli, she bonked her head rather than drop him, prompting me to wonder if it was fair to relegate administrative tasks and baby-care to a woman who was nine months pregnant.

"I want us to nurse each other's babies," Anastasia said.

"Okay," I said, immediately.

"They'll be milk-siblings," she said excitedly.

"Yeah," I said. "Wow."

What I didn't do was yell, "OMIGOD! THAT IS SO BIZARRE THAT YOU WANT TO DO THAT!" But that was my first internal reaction. Second internal reaction: *How am I going to get out of this when I already said okay?*

The issue for me seemed clear. It was one of health. You can't let other babies drink your milk. Skuli certainly couldn't drink her milk. I practiced in my head how I would explain that to her. *Anastasia, my milk is specially formulated with antibodies perfectly designed just for Skuli . . .* But then the whole history of wet nurses popped into my head—obviously babies can and do drink other mothers' milk.

On the web, both the Centers for Disease Control and La Leche League discourage "cross-nursing"—both citing the possibility that either mother might have serious communicable diseases. (Many diseases, including HIV, hepatitis, and syphilis, can be transmitted by human breastmilk.) But neither of us has any of those diseases. So I called my father, who is a doctor and not a hippie, to see if there were any medical reasons not to let a healthy friend nurse your baby. "None that I can think of," he said matter-of-factly.

Oh. At that point, I had to face facts about my own relationship to health consciousness: I didn't alter my diet or quit drinking based on being a nursing mom, and I was no poster child for hale living, existing as I do on coffee, seltzer, and candied cashews. According to La Leche League, I shouldn't even be giving my own child my tainted milk, let alone another woman's.

So, maybe the problem was more an issue of being normal, decent parents. What if we did cross-nurse and people found out? What if our children found out?! I felt deep shame at the thought of telling anyone we had done it. Surely we would be identified as gross and perverted, the parenting equivalent of wife-swappers. Anastasia was sort of the Angelina Jolie type in my friend group, so she could possibly pull this off, but I was more Gwyneth—superficially serene, but essentially uptight. Why did Anastasia want to do this? She asked and I was so flabbergasted, I agreed. After all, she had vacuumed my apartment.

I worried about the milk-siblings offer for a few days, and then called Amy Richards. Amy is very logical. She'd know what to do in this situation. "My instinct is that Anastasia sees nursing each other's babies as a way for you two to bond," she told me. "You're very close and this is an expression of that intimacy." Amy's take was so different from the hysterical rant in my head, I at once felt more relaxed. "If you don't want to do it, I think you can just acknowledge how beautiful it is that you are so close," continued Amy. "And you don't have to let her nurse Skuli to demonstrate that." Just hearing Amy frame it as bonding took the pressure off of me and with that, some of the judgmental thoughts I'd been having about Anastasia. *If anything,* I thought, *my resistance is more of a limitation on my part—I should just own up to that. We are close. I can tell her that I'm just not comfortable with our kids being milk-siblings.*

Soon after our conversation, Anastasia had her son. Her delivery didn't go at all as she'd planned. She had a midwife and a doula and a birthing ball, but after three days of stalling labor, she had an emergency C-section and was utterly flattened by the experience. Her boyfriend, who had practiced for months to coach her through natural childbirth, didn't know what to do to help his shivering, shell-shocked partner. She lay there on her side after having her stomach and uterus stitched back up, but when her doula brought her son in and rolled him onto her breast, he latched on and began sucking hard. Just like that, she started to heal from the difficulty of the past three days. Anastasia's luck—even talent—with nursing held. She could squirt milk into Lionel's mouth from several inches away, like a fountain. She could nurse standing up, talking on the phone, and while making homemade ravioli. Meanwhile, I had to "get into position"—propping up a pillow and cupping my breast as if screwing together a pipe—for several weeks before nursing was even remotely casual.

A few months after Lionel was born, I returned from a particularly draining two weeks on book tour with Skuli. I had lurched past the point of looking slim again after pregnancy and was scarecrow-thin, with staticky hair and a zitty complexion that bespoke red-eye flights and Starbucks dining. I sunk into an armchair at her apartment, watching gratefully as she effortlessly entertained Skuli. She listened sympathetically as I told her boring tales of the book tour. Then, just as she was bringing me fresh coffee and making Skuli laugh, I was overcome by how fortunate I was that we were friends and could share this parenting experience. Lionel began crying from his room. "Hey," I said suddenly, when she returned with him, "we never did that nursing thing you mentioned back before Lionel was born."

"I know," she said.

"Maybe I'll nurse him right now," I said, feeling sort of vulnerable in the offering, as if I was actually the weird Angelina friend. "If that sounds okay to you."

"Well, I just read Lionel's horoscope and it said he was going to get nourishment from exotic sources this week," Anastasia said. "So that would make his horoscope true."

I took him and rearranged my shirt and bra to expose my breast. Skuli sat on the floor, not seeming to think anything weird was going on. I put Lionel on my nipple and he began sucking. The familiar tug made the milk rush in; his sucking strength and style were different than Skuli's, his little face so incredibly sweet. It felt really . . . normal. Anastasia fed Skuli, too, and because he was older and had teeth, she got her first bite.

A few months later, over drinks and a bit tipsy in that way that makes me confess everything, I revealed to another friend, Gillian, that Skuli and Lionel were milk-siblings. "You're kidding," she said.

"No," I said. "It's true."

"I'm so jealous," she said. "I was too afraid to bring that up to any of my friends."

—Originally published in *Babble,* January 2007

EPILOGUE

This piece takes the cake for generating the most press of any piece I have ever written, which is especially ironic since I spent very little time writing it and am hardly a cross-nursing activist, seeing as how I used formula right away and stopped breastfeeding at all after seven months. Still, as soon as the piece went live, I was called by at least a dozen media outlets, from *The Wall Street Journal* to the *New York Post,* and the piece was blogged about everywhere from Gawker to Gothamist. The online comments sections expressed titillation, support, outrage, revulsion, interest, and more than one prediction of the enormity of Skuli's future therapy bills based on this experience of cross-nursing. A few intrepid commenters pointed out that Anastasia and I had been a couple in our early twenties, as if to prove that breastfeeding each other's babies was just a new way to make out together. Most curious to me were the people who held tenaciously to the idea that cross-feeding was like sleeping with your friend's husband. That is, nursing another person's baby, unless it was a dire emergency, was undeniably sexual or cheating on your baby.

I don't deny that breasts can have a role in sex, but I have come to believe that breastmilk is, more than anything else, food. The breast as handy conveyance for the milk is probably only as erotic when used for another baby as it is when you feed your own child. After all, some women describe feeling turned-on when nursing their baby; others feel relaxation, minor irritation, or just relief that something so portable reliably shuts the baby up. I wasn't at this place of calm understanding of the true nature of breastmilk when Anastasia first asked me to cross-nurse, as evidenced by my panicky reaction. But, having had the opportunity to examine my assumptions, it's clear that breastmilk is a bodily fluid—like blood or saliva—but critically different in that it is also plain old nutrition. Moreover, breastfeeding is many wonderful things, but it can also be tiring and a burden. Having a loved one in your life that can feed your child easily is, to me, a boon.

Cross-nursing isn't the only breastfeeding practice that provokes derisive snorts and horror. Nursing a child who is old enough to ask to be fed or unbutton your blouse is also shameful. There are strict rules when it comes to breastfeeding if you want societal approbation—breastfeed for one year. If you can't or don't want to, prepare to feel inadequate. If you have tons of milk and love to feed your child that way, prepare to be called a freak who is presumed to be nursing for selfish reasons and will create a weird, babyish child.

Even several years after writing this initial piece, I still field calls from reporters trying to do stories on the "trend" of cross-nursing. I always question whether it's a trend if Anastasia and I are the only people reporters and producers can find who have done it—and we only did it with Skuli and Lionel two times. On the other hand, through my own calling around, I easily found ten women, not friends of mine and most in the birthing and doula world, who had breastfed another's baby. Most didn't mention it too often, largely because it is seen as violating an enormous taboo, and most of us don't need that kind of condemnation in our lives.

Lionel and Skuli—both six years old at this writing—remain best friends. Their bond is delightful and deep, nourished by true friendship and intimacy and adventures together. I guess they really are "breast friends." Anastasia and I have each had another baby boy since the *Babble* article was originally published. Yes, we cross-nursed.

WHY WE SPEAK OUT
WHEN WE SPEAK OUT

In 1962, Sherri Finkbine, a star of TV's *Romper Room* and a mild-mannered, thirty-year-old mother of four, found herself at the center of a maelstrom around abortion. Her doctor told her, pregnant with her fifth child, that the baby would very likely be severely deformed because she had taken thalidomide during her pregnancy. He recommended a "therapeutic" abortion, then done quietly by many doctors and hospitals following this kind of diagnosis.

Hoping to warn women about the dangers of this drug and help others in her position, Finkbine went public with her story. That was her first mistake. The doctors could operate freely only under the cover of silence, so her abortion had to be a secret. Now, in the light of day, a media firestorm provoked death threats against her and her family. The hospital, fearing the controversy, canceled her procedure. On August 17, 1962, Sheri Finkbine traveled to Sweden; the next day, she underwent her therapeutic abortion.

Finkbine was one of the first significant instances of a woman's going on record to say, "I had an abortion." That simple declaration is one of the hardest, most vulnerable things a person can utter. Over time, women's speaking up and out about their own abortions has played a pivotal role in changing the law and the world as we know it today. For these women, the personal was political. I would one day find myself among them.

Abortion—legal or illegal, dirty or clean—has long magnetized women to feminism. In the early days of the women's liberation movement, ladies found each other and the movement by telling the truth about their abortions. Even Gloria Steinem didn't realize she was a feminist until she attended a hearing in a church basement where women were testifying about their own abortions. That historic event, on March 21, 1969, was staged by the New York-based feminist group Redstockings. To give you an idea of what they were up against in that era, a previous hearing the Redstockings had disrupted featured a panel of twelve men and one woman—a nun. These young feminists declared themselves the "real experts" on abortion because, as women, they were in danger of unwanted pregnancy and had actually experienced abortion.

Rosalyn Baxandall spoke first. She was terrified. When she got home, her grandmother called, having seen Ros on the news, and said, "You've had an *abortion?*" As Ros confirmed the information and braced herself to be scolded, her grandmother said, "Well, I have had six!" By April 1970, New York state passed the most liberal abortion laws in the country, beating *Roe v. Wade* by nearly three years.

On April 5, 1971, the French weekly newsmagazine *Le Nouvel Observateur* published the "Manifesto of the 343," a petition of 343 French women, including Simone de Beauvoir, Catherine Deneuve, Jeanne Moreau, and Monique Wittig, declaring that they had all had abortions. A year later, *Ms.* magazine's debut issue featured a similar "I Had an Abortion" petition, signed by fifty-three well-known women, including Gloria Steinem and Billie Jean King.

Less than a year after the *Ms.* petition, on January 22, 1973, *Roe v. Wade* was handed down, legalizing abortion through the first trimester (and with restrictions in the second) in all states.[1] On January 22, 2003, the thirtieth anniversary of *Roe,* Patricia Beninato was so frustrated that every time she turned on the television, she saw anti-choicers claiming that having an abortion leads directly to clinical depression that she decided to create ImNotSorry.net—a space for women to say that they've had abortions and aren't going to apologize for it.

In the fall of 2003, I found Beninato and Baxandall—and all the women before them who had the courage to share their abortion experience—very inspiring. I'd never even been pregnant, but on January 22, 2004, feeling emboldened, I launched the I Had an Abortion Project. The first step was distributing T-shirts printed with the words I HAD AN ABORTION. At an event at the feminist bookstore Bluestockings, I invited women and men to come out about their abortion experiences. My friend, the filmmaker Gillian Aldrich, and I began interviewing women who'd had abortions for a film called *I Had an Abortion.* I wanted to destigmatize the experience, to point out that women who've had abortions aren't awful women we don't know; they are our mothers, sisters, aunts, friends, wives, and selves.

The next month, I was pregnant with my first son, and by the time Rush Limbaugh and Matt Drudge publicized the fact that Planned Parenthood was selling the T-shirt, I was seven months along. The publicity (Limbaugh and Drudge led to Fox, CNN, and dozens of other outlets) provoked both a run on the shirts (hundreds sold

---

1. The plaintiff, Jane Roe, was Norma McCorvey, who sought an abortion but couldn't get one. In her life, she had at least three pregnancies and gave birth to three daughters, none of whom she got to raise, culminating in the *Roe* baby. Thus, the most famous person associated with legal abortion apparently never had one.

overnight) and a painful debate over whether the shirt was brave and important or callous and cheap. (I think the shirt is potentially quite brave and important; certainly I advocate using casual "everyday" spaces to discuss critical and silenced issues.)

I was inundated with stories from women about their abortions and their lives. I heard mainly from people who were grateful to have something to honor an experience they were told they had to keep secret. Women on Waves, Dutch doctor Rebecca Gomperts's radical project to provide abortions in international waters, created its own I HAD AN ABORTION T-shirts and bulletproof dresses as part of a larger art project about abortion. The project's mission statement declared its hope that by "making the reality of abortion visible, change will be catalyzed."

Our *I Had an Abortion* film debuted on the *Roe* anniversary in 2005. The film featured ten women and ten funny, sad, frank, and complex stories of having a reproductive system and being female. I learned how diverse women's experiences of abortion are—depending on many factors, including where they are in their lives when the pregnancy occurs. In 2007, two other documentaries, *Silent Choices* (Faith Pennick's film about black women's abortion experiences) and *The Abortion Diaries* (Penny Lane's short centering on her own abortion as a teenager), began screening around the country, to great acclaim and gratitude from women and men.

And then the political became personal for me.

On March 22, 2010, three months after Angie Jackson, a twenty-seven-year-old mother in Florida, live-tweeted her abortion with RU-486 (causing another media firestorm), I bought a pregnancy test. My son Magnus was almost eight months; Skuli was five and a half. I would be forty in two months and was just getting my brain back and a handle on my responsibilities since I'd gotten knocked up seventeen months earlier.

I felt trepidacious. My period, which normally came about every three weeks, was late. I was a little edgy. My sense of smell was extra strong. I felt dizzy sitting on the couch watching the Tiger Woods *South Park* with my boyfriend. I wasn't sure when the right time was to take a test, given that I knew I probably would not want to continue with the pregnancy. It was really the pregnancy more than anything else, I realized, that weighed on me. I could pretty happily imagine a little daughter named Effie gamboling around at age two in a ruffled dress, but I couldn't imagine spending the next eight months feeling alternatingly nauseous and like a whale, followed by the rigors of birth, and then sleep deprivation as we got to know our newborn.

Maybe I'm just late, I thought to myself as I bought the test. *And it's better to know so I can be relieved and marvel at how paranoid I am—or figure this out.* So, around 6:00 PM on a Sunday, while my boyfriend, BD, made bratwursts and salad and I showered Skuli and got Magpie into his PJs, I found time to pee on the stick. "Is that a tampon?" asked Skuli, in the bathroom with me, as always. "Gross."

Within seconds, the little boxes began showing their Polaroid news: a little +. Positive. Pregnant. Normally, I considered that positive. This time, it felt wrong—not devastatingly sad or tragic, just something I couldn't bear doing right then in my life.

The conversation with BD was wistful; he'd like more children. I was already having trouble meeting my obligations at work and with Skuli and Magnus. I didn't want to offer my body to that process again.

I called my OB's office at 9:00 AM, Monday. The nurse, Sally, called back to tell me "*no one* in the practice performs abortions." This surprised me. Had I never inquired whether my doctor was pro-choice? Then Dr. G, my actual doctor, called back to say that actually Dr. K, who delivered Magnus and who was in their practice, *did* do abortions. Suddenly, I remembered a conversation I'd had with Dr. K right after Magnus came out. She had asked me what I did, and I'd said I mainly wrote about abortion; she'd said she did them and was really committed to providing them.

I made an appointment with Dr. K for Friday, March 26. That day, I went to her office at 1:00 PM and filled out paperwork. The receptionist was warm. I went into the examining room, was weighed, and had my blood pressure taken. Dr. K examined my uterus and did a pap culture and an internal sonogram. Back in her office, surrounded by drawings by her daughters, she gave me Mifeprex, otherwise known as RU-486—the "abortion pill." I swallowed the pill and felt . . . totally fine. Dr. K told me I would be good to go all night—no need to change my plans. "Really?" I asked, assuming I should lie in bed and read *Play It as It Lays*. "You'll feel how you feel right now," she said. "Tomorrow's the bad part."

I went to the pharmacy to get Vicodin, an antibiotic, and misoprostol, which, taken the next day, would start the contractions that would expel the contents of my uterus. The pharmacist—I don't think I imagined this—glared at me and dropped the misoprostol on the counter. "That's for that woman *in trouble*," she muttered to her colleague. "What?" I said, feeling like I almost wanted to fight with her.

That night, I went out to dinner with friends and to a Spoon concert at Radio City. The next morning, I took the misoprostol. My plan had been to go hear Susan Faludi and Jack Halberstam speak at The New School and then take the pills, but I decided to get it over with earlier in the day. Until early 2006, women could take this drug vaginally, but due to increased instances of infection, it was now administered buccally. I dissolved the six pills in my cheeks for an hour and then swallowed the mess down with water. I took a Vicodin and got in bed.

Then came hours of contractions muted by painkillers, lots of blood and tissue, and the sweetness of getting to sleep during the day. By dinnertime, I was up and showered. A few days later, most of the blood had passed, though the bleeding lingered for nearly two weeks, like an extra-long period. After many years of connecting to complex emotions around ending a pregnancy, I wondered if I might have regret. I was surprised and relieved by how simple—emotionally and physically—the abortion had been.

"We have to give women healthy spaces to talk about their abortions," Steph Herold, a twentysomething reproductive justice activist, told me in the fall of 2010. She had just launched the hashtag #ihadanabortion on Twitter, and the media was once again fanning the flames of controversy. Was Twitter an appropriate medium in which to talk about something so serious? Wasn't this need to talk about one's abortion simply a sign of a generation devoted to oversharing? Herold answered no, and smartly placed her own decision to speak out within a history of speaking out.

Today, women and men who share their abortion experiences do so in a different environment. Abortion is legal, so it doesn't have the same historic impact that Sherri Finkbine's or the Redstockings' speak-outs had. Yet after several decades of speak-outs and attempts to come out about abortion, the stigma remains, proving that the high emotions around this issue aren't neutralized so easily. Despite this difficulty, a profound purpose remains in speaking out. When each of us does so, abortion history transforms into a beautiful and rich collective memoir.

"I had an abortion" is important for me to say because I stand shoulder to shoulder with other women, people who believe in the right of all human beings to make decisions about their bodies and lives. Most important, I say I had an abortion out loud because my life is no shameful secret.

Q&A

Loretta Ross

ATLANTA-BASED SECOND WAVE FEMINIST LORETTA ROSS

is arguably the most significant figure in the modern repro-rights movement. This "reproductive justice" strategy, articulated by women of color, de-emphasizes labels like "pro-choice" and "pro-life" and focuses on an affirmative role for government in ensuring that women can access their reproductive rights.

Loretta was born in Temple, Texas, on August 16, 1953, the sixth of eight kids of a conservative, military father and a strict Southern Baptist mother. Amid that bustle, she learned early on to speak up if she wanted to be heard. In the forty years she has been working in women's liberation, she has coauthored a book, been the executive director of the first rape crisis center in the United States, and served as director of women of color programs for the National Organization for Women, organizing the first national conference on Women of Color and Reproductive Rights in 1987.

Loretta inspires countless younger feminists and womanists with her ability to include conflicting feelings and beliefs in her theories, so as

to include a broader range of women. In 2007, with her son and grandson in the audience, Loretta got her BA from Agnes Scott College, completing an education started in 1970. Now the national coordinator for SisterSong Women of Color Reproductive Justice Collective, Loretta is getting her PhD in gender studies, finishing an anthology about reproductive justice, and touring the country as a powerful, riveting speaker. We met in 2003 in the lead up to the March for Women's Lives. I was immediately struck by her natural charisma as well as her ability to make complicated political theories utterly understandable. Loretta is one of the ten women featured in the I Had an Abortion documentary. In the film, as in life, she's both brutally honest and radically compassionate.

Jennifer: Do you remember what your entry point was for any sort of activism?

Loretta: Well, there was the conscious experience and the unconscious experience. The unconscious: When I was fourteen, I became pregnant through incest. An older cousin thought that, rather than baby-sitting me, it was a better idea to have sex with me. He was twenty-seven at the time.

J: Do you remember at the time feeling like there was any way to get him not to do that?

L: Well, to be honest, I was what we now call one of those "Red Lobster girls." A lot of adult male predators use the bait of dates and dinners at places like Red Lobster to get sexual favors from very young and impressionable girls. I was an early Red Lobster girl—even though my cousin took me to all the nightclubs in Los Angeles, rather than Red Lobster.

I thought I was having the summer of my life—I was being treated as an adult, going to all these places my mother wouldn't let me go, getting dressed up and plied with liquor. The bubble burst when I became pregnant. I told him and he literally left the state.

J: This was before abortion was legal?

L: This was 1968, years before *Roe*. We lived in Texas and heard rumors of girls going to Mexico for abortions; very few of them came back, so we didn't consider abortion a viable option. So the plan was conceived by my parents for me to be placed in a home for unwed mothers. I would have the baby and give him up for adoption, which actually suited me fine, because I had no intention of becoming a parent that way—through incest.

J: What do you remember about being at the home for unwed mothers?

L: It was a horrible experience. It was in San Antonio, near Trinity University. We were locked behind huge, high gates, never allowed to leave the compound. We were the servants; we did all the cooking, cleaning, and maintenance of the facility. Of thirty girls, I was the only black girl. I was there for three months. It was a time of deep isolation. My parents never visited. We got up every morning about six o'clock and prayed for our sins and then went to breakfast; we did work and then we prayed some more. In the afternoon, tutors would show up, because we were all in high school or junior high school. Then dinner and lights out by about seven or eight o'clock at night. No television, no music, nothing to liven the place. It was pretty dreary.

J: What happened after you gave birth?

L: My sister was with me; my mother wouldn't come. In the hospital, they brought my son out to me and I saw something I didn't expect: He had my face. I kept panting over and over again, "He's got my face, he's got my face." I couldn't go through with the adoption. So that's how I became a parent.

I had a scholarship to Radcliffe. The Ivy League schools headhunted the brightest black kids at the time to satisfy their quotas. My high school counselor had nominated me for the scholarship, but when she learned that I had a baby, she wrote Radcliffe and they rescinded the scholarship.

J: You just spoke in a very emotional way about seeing your son, but what do you think gave you the strength to defy what everyone was telling you to do, and even what you thought was the best thing to do?

L: I don't want to sugarcoat my motivations. I wonder how much of that strength was formed by the mother love, the child-mother bonding, and how much it was plain old, very common adolescent rebellion. My mother really couldn't handle my pregnancy. I didn't learn until many, many years later that my mother had been a victim of child sexual abuse from age eight to sixteen. The fact that she went ballistic over my pregnancy made sense once I knew her history, but at the time, I didn't know.

J: Had she also had a pregnancy as a result of incest?

L: No, not that I know of. I don't think so. She got married at sixteen to escape from an uncle. My mother didn't tell me about her own sexual abuse history until I started working at the rape crisis center a few years later.

J: I want to leap forward to the "conscious" part of your growth as an activist.

L: The *conscious* part of my political life happened in 1970, at college. I read *The Diary of Malcolm X* and *The Black Woman,* by Toni Cade, that year. I also became pregnant because my mother would not sign the parental consent form for me to access birth control; she thought that I would not engage in sexual activity even though I was thousands of miles away from home. There wasn't any sex education at my school and she still had not figured out how to talk to me about sex. I think she just hoped for abstinence, which was difficult for a child already sexualized by an adult. Fortunately for me, Washington, D.C., legalized abortion in 1970 before *Roe v. Wade*. I went to a hospital for a very late-term abortion, because it was so complicated getting the parental consent form from my mother—my sister eventually forged her name—and for my boyfriend to raise the money. Separate from that, I was the freshman class vice president and an activist kind of soul already.

J: You were already a leader.

L: I was always mouthy. I was captain of the debate team in junior high. I started the girls' drill team when I was in high school because the boys had a team and the girls didn't. I can't really describe that as feminist consciousness, but more like feminist unconsciousness.

J: Was your son with you while you were in college?

L: My parents raised him until I dropped out after three years, when the rules about out-of-state tuition changed because of President Nixon. My mother and I had a very turbulent relationship at that time. I was coming into adulthood and she was having difficulty recognizing that. I represented her very problematic past, with the incest and the sexual abuse story, which was very painful and she hadn't ever talked to anyone about. Looking back on it, I can be more sympathetic than I could at the time I was living through it.

J: How did you become part of DC Rape Crisis, the first rape crisis center in the country?

L: My son and I had a studio apartment in Adams Morgan in Washington, D.C. I got a notice one day that we had sixty days to move, because they were converting the apartments to condominiums. Some tenants and I decided to meet in the laundry room to fight the eviction. I volunteered to take notes, and the next thing I knew, I was the president of my tenants' association. At a Citywide Housing Coalition meeting, I met this woman Nkenge Toure, who had been in the Black Panther Party. She invited me to come volunteer at the DC Rape Crisis Center. I remember snapping, "I don't want to go work with those white women." Nkenge looked at me and said, "Sister, would I lead you wrong?" I was too intimidated to pro-test—who's going to say no to a Black Panther? Nkenge was the second executive director of the DC Rape Crisis Center and was responsible for my formal introduction to the women's movement.

J: What was the movement like in the late '70s?

L: At the time, Washington was a hotbed of feminist—and especially black feminist—activism. *Off Our Backs* and *Aegis*—which was a feminist activist magazine—were founded during that time. The D.C. Area Feminist Alliance, the National Organization for Women, black health feminists came up from Gainesville, Florida . . . All of this was just bubbling around me at the time. I was in the right place at the right time. I just went along for the ride because it was the most exciting thing that had happened to me.

J: Did feminism shed new light on your own experiences? It did for me.

L: That involvement in feminism explained to me all the things that had hap-pened to me in my life. My story was at the intersection of reproductive violence and sexual violence.

J: And how did making sense of those early experiences help you?

L: I credit the feminist movement for bringing me back from the brink of suicide. That's what many people in my situation end up doing—that or self-medication or drug abuse. That's what the women's movement brought me back from: the brink of all those things.

J: You were literally suicidal?

L: That was not a metaphor. I eventually took the advice I gave others and got some therapy. I was politically conscious and self-destructive at the same time. I'm still dealing with it. I'm overweight, and that's part of it.

J: Let's talk about the movement's transformation from reproductive rights to reproductive justice, your role, and the role of other women of color in that, and its implications.

L: Reproductive justice represents a convergence of events. In 1994 there was an international conference on population and development in Cairo. At the same time, Hillary Clinton was engaged in healthcare reform, but made the same mistake Obama has by excluding abortion. Black women activists observed that, internationally, women were using the human rights framework to claim the same rights that we were arguing for under the constitutional framework, using the anti-government frame, which is the right to privacy. Internationally, women were arguing they had the human right to food, clothing, shelter, and family planning, among other things. In Cairo, feminists won acknowledgment that one cannot talk about population without talking about development; that the ability of any woman to control what happens to her body is directly related to the community in which she's embedded. You cannot push family planning on a community that lacks basic access to healthcare.

J: Right, abortion and birth control are part of healthcare, but they aren't healthcare.

L: As women of color, we were used to just caucusing at the white women's conferences; we didn't have our own independent space to talk in. After Cairo, at the Illinois Pro-Choice Alliance, someone said, "The basic problem is that abortion is isolated from other social justice issues, but it's those other social justice issues that determine whether the woman has the baby or not." We organized a group of black women to purchase an ad

in *The Washington Post* about healthcare reform in 1994. We called ourselves Women of African Descent for Reproductive Justice. We said we
did not want healthcare reform that did not include reproductive healthcare services and abortion. About four hundred women signed the ad.

**J: That was the moment this crucial term was coined, with that group
of women?**

L: Yes. We spliced "reproductive rights" together with "social justice" and
came up with the term "reproductive justice," signifying the embedding
of abortion rights within a social justice framework. We had our first
national conference in 2003. Our plenary session asked, what does looking at abortion rights through a social justice lens look like? We had
Byllye Avery, Asian women, and women of all different races coming to
talk about reproductive justice. In 2004, Asians and Pacific Islanders for
Reproductive Health became Asian Communities for Reproductive Justice. It was the first organization to use the term in its name. SisterSong
began using it in 2005. And then we pushed it down the throats of the
organizers of the last big abortion march.

**J: In 2004, leading up to the march, we were at a *Glamour* meeting
together, and I remember the original name of the march was the
March for Choice, or something like that.**

L: It was called the March for Freedom of Choice.

**J: Right, and then organizations like SisterSong said, "We can't organize
under that banner."**

L: Silvia Henriquez [head of the National Latina Institute for Reproductive Health], a SisterSong member at the time, called me and said,
"Loretta, we have to decide what to do about this March for Freedom
of Choice." I told Silvia, "I'm not working with those white women." It
wasn't because I dislike white women; it was because I had been on

the NOW staff for five years—I had organized women of color for the march in '86 and '89—and I was convinced that we needed to build SisterSong to pay attention to the needs of women of color. This ain't the time to drop our agenda to go run to their agenda again, you know? They didn't ask our permission to march. I thought, *Let them march; let us stay focused on what we're doing, which is building this movement for women of color, please.*

But Silvia was insistent, and, not wanting to upset her, I said, "Okay. Why don't we invite them to come to SisterSong and tell us why we should endorse the march? I have only one stipulation: They have to send a woman of color to address us." Two of the four lead organizations could not.

J: **The four were the Feminist Majority Foundation, Planned Parenthood, NOW, and NARAL Pro-Choice America.**

L: And two of those organizations didn't have any women of color on staff above office manager, which, in my mind, kind of indicated that they weren't ready to have this talk anyway. After thirty years of women of color constantly complaining about their lack of diversity, they still weren't ready.

We had six hundred women of color at this, our first, conference. The representatives from the big four made their pitch for why we needed to march against the Bush Administration, march for abortion rights, blah blah blah. Then we opened the mic. People reacted to the fact that here's these mainstream organizations asking us to work on their march, but what had they done for us lately? We've self-organized without your help—now you want our help, right? I became the point person to negotiate with them. I actually thought that if I raised our demands so high, they would go away.

I demanded three things: a name change, money to buy out our time from our organizations while we organized on behalf of theirs, and women of color on the steering committee.

J: And they met the demands, right? I know the name was changed from March for Freedom of Choice to March for Women's Lives.

L: All demands were met. After that, Alice Cohan [at the Feminist Majority Foundation] asked me if I would be codirector. I felt she'd called my bluff. That's how I ended up being march codirector and working around the country to convince women to come to the march. The event itself was wildly successful. We had 1.15 million people, the largest protest march in American history.

J: Younger women appear to me to be much more conversant with the vocabulary of reproductive justice, whereas a couple of years I felt there was more of a resistance among big organizations to using that terminology. Now I think there's much more adoption, because a whole new generation is coming-of-age to whom that language speaks.

L: Well, part of it is co-option, to be honest. The mainstream groups are taking that phrase without taking what is packed in it. I mean, "reproductive justice" is just the U.S.'s way of saying "human rights that are intersectional, universal, and unalienable." If you aren't using the human rights framework as your legal strategy, using the phrase "reproductive justice" is empty. It's meaningless.

J: It's an attempt for organizations to indicate that they are inclusive of women of color.

L: That's the other thing: There is racism in how the term is used—as if it is just for women of color. The theory was *created* by women of color, but that doesn't mean it only applies to women of color. White women need human rights too! Reproductive justice is the application of the human rights framework to reproductive politics in the US.

J: One of the core things about reproductive justice is that it has an affirmative role for government, whereas reproductive rights says, "Government, get out of my life." Can you talk a little about this?

L: When you call on the human rights framework, there are things that the government shouldn't do, but there are other things that the government *must* do. The government can't tell you whether or not to have a baby, but it has to ensure that you have the means to have or not have a baby in an environment that is safe, that is affordable and accessible. I compare it to an airplane ride: The government can't tell me to fly. It can't tell me where to go. But when I do choose to fly, it has an obligation to make sure that plane is safe and doesn't come plummeting out of the sky. It has regulations to make sure the airfare is affordable so these airlines can't charge anything they want for a ticket. It has to make sure the airports are accessible so that these smaller markets aren't just shut down because the airlines only want to service D.C., New York, and Los Angeles. Safe, affordable, accessible is the role of government in enabling its citizens to enact private decisions.

J: I can already hear people saying, "But that's pro-choice, that's the existing model." Why *not* use the term "pro-choice"?

L: This framework is not interchangeable with pro-choice. We think "pro-choice" is a great phrase. We wish all women had choices. But not all women do because of healthcare disparities, immigration policies, racism, homophobia, etc. Moreover, the pro-choice framework does not demand an affirmative role for government, just a negative one—"Keep your laws off my body"—that is understandably necessary given how conservatives want to regulate everything that occurs in our bedrooms. I read the other day about a Florida politician astutely analyzing the current conservative approach: Small government for the regulation of businesses and big government for the regulation of women.

J: So, reproductive justice is a precursor to choice. What's going to happen with the reproductive justice framework? Will it become something the big organizations eventually manifest?

L: I think reproductive justice is going to supplant the pro-choice frame eventually. It's more viable and brings more diverse people into the conversation and it works across movements—bringing new activists and new leadership. Young people in particular resonate with the reproductive justice framework because they live in a much more intersectional and interconnected way and better understand the importance of building a human rights movement in the United States that holds our own country accountable to its people.

—Interviewed on December 16, 2010

WHEN MOM AND DAD DON'T KNOW WHAT'S BEST

Twenty-nine years ago, I helped my teenage sister get an abortion, without telling our parents. Today her story is still proof to me that parental consent laws don't work.

I grew up the second of three daughters in a pro-choice household in Fargo, North Dakota. Our family talked about politics, read *Our Bodies, Ourselves* and voted Democrat, but when it came to actually discussing sex, my parents' mantra was "high school is too young."

In 1985, the summer after my freshman year in high school, my 16-year-old sister told me she was pregnant. Andrea, a National Merit Scholar, knew two things: She wanted an abortion and she didn't want to tell mom and dad.

"I'll help you," I said, honored that she'd turned to me.

Andrea wasn't worried that my parents would throw her out or beat her. She, like many minors who become pregnant, was more concerned about preserving her relationship with her family.

"I remember feeling like I can't add this to the official roster of things I've done," Andrea told me recently. "I was too young emotionally to have sex, but physically I wasn't. Any conversation I would have had with mom and dad would have ended with them telling me not to do it." She didn't want them to know anything about what felt to her like "a big mistake."

Andrea had $60 saved from her job at Burger King. I helped her raise the additional $200 she needed by borrowing it from an acquaintance at school. Although North Dakota had had an abortion clinic since 1980, there was also a law, in place since 1981, stipulating that both parents consent to a minor's abortion. Andrea went through the process of getting a judicial bypass. The clinic steered her though an interview with an amenable judge, I got her the money just in time, and Andrea got her abortion. Although the experience was difficult for her, we were rather proud that we'd gone through it alone.

I've thought about Andrea's story a lot lately, especially now that California—which, like New York, generally has very liberal abortion laws—is considering its first parental notification legislation. Missouri and other states are considering laws that would make it a crime to even counsel a girl about her options. Some thirty-three states enforce parental consent or notification laws. In fact, it is the most popular restriction among people who support *Roe v. Wade.* A recent poll by the Pew Research Center (released August 3, 2005) found that 73 percent of Americans supported some form of required parental consent. When asked why, people often cite the fact that a minor can't have a wisdom tooth removed without parental consent, so why should she be allowed to have an abortion on her own?

But Andrea's story always seemed proof to me that parental consent laws—logical as they may sound—don't work. If a girl doesn't want to tell her parents, she won't, even if they are nice and pro-choice.

By necessity, many clinics know how to efficiently work around the restriction of parental notification. Jane Bovard, the clinic director of the Red River Women's Clinic, who helped Andrea get her judicial bypass, told me she has never been turned down in twenty-five years of doing about two judicial bypasses a week. But many judges aren't so willing, and in states where bypasses aren't easy to come by, clinic workers are more likely to see a girl ask her boyfriend to beat her abdomen with a baseball bat (as in a recent Michigan case), than to see an increase in minors telling their parents. Bovard estimates that 80 percent of the minors she has worked with do tell their parents. The law mandating that they do so hasn't changed that statistic.

"If you are looking at fourteen-year-olds or younger, it's almost universal that they include their parents," Peg Johnston, another longtime clinician, told me.

Johnston is the clinic director at Southern Tier Women's Services in Binghamton, New York, and a founder and director of the Abortion Conversation Project (ACP). She says, "I appreciate the New York State legislature's willingness to stay out of parental consent laws. State law says if you are old enough to get pregnant, you are already a mother, to some extent, and you get to choose what course your life will take." She continues: "Having said that, it is a crisis and these young women need all of the support that they can get. Unfortunately, government statutes tend to be punitive, not supportive."

ACP is working on a campaign called "Mom, Dad, I'm Pregnant" to help parents and kids talk to each other during this kind of crisis and to encourage open communication. The Reverend Becky Turner of Missouri's Religious Coalition for Reproductive

Choice gave me advice more powerful than any law. When her own daughter was about fourteen, Turner accompanied her to a routine gynecology appointment and told the gynecologist she wanted her to write in her daughter's chart that regardless of what the law is at the time, she can treat her daughter as an adult patient.

"I said: 'I hope she will feel comfortable coming to me, but if for any reason she doesn't, I want you to please give her what she needs. If she needs birth control, give it to her; if she needs an abortion referral, please make it and don't feel like you need to call me for permission.' I think, as a result of that, she tells me more than I want to know," says Turner, laughing, "but it's my moment that I am most proud of as a parent."

Andrea did eventually tell our mother, who told our father. Our parents weren't mad at her; they were heartsick and frustrated with me, too, for helping. I remember being angry that they didn't appreciate why I'd helped her rather than turn to them. It took me a long time to begin to understand how devastating being excluded from Andrea's pregnancy and abortion was to them. I'm still honored that Andrea turned to me, and grateful that she was able to get the abortion she wanted. But all these years later, in a time when abortion is, if anything, more stigmatized, I want to do anything I can to help girls and parents turn to each other—willingly.

—Originally published with *Alternet,* September 2005

EPILOGUE

My understanding of abortion politics has deepened and evolved with each passing year. I now openly acknowledge that I think the fetus is a life and that, for some, the taking of that life is traumatic. I can see more clearly how birth control and abortion can be deployed as a replacement for healthcare for impoverished women, and how that is far from reproductive "freedom." One thing that has proven to be true, even as I learn more that provides nuance to my opinions about abortion, is that restrictions are, in a word, bad. They put medical decisions in the hands of (often male) legislators. Restrictions rarely cause someone to rethink having an abortion but rather make it so she has a later term, more expensive procedure.

Parental consent laws are particularly vexing, because they sound so logical. "If a girl has to consult her parents before getting her wisdom teeth pulled, certainly she should consult them for an abortion," a friend's father once boomed at me. "It's serious!" But removing an unwanted pregnancy is different than extracting unwanted teeth. A pregnancy, unlike molars, invokes crucial elements of one's identity: religion, self-image, relationship to family, and relationship to the person who helped conceive the pregnancy. Parental consent laws, often meant to help identify statutory rape or sexual abuse, don't readily acknowledge incest and abuse by parents. As of May 2011, thirty-five states enforce parental consent or notification laws. According the Guttmacher Institute, the gold standard for statistics about reproductive issues, teenagers are more likely than older women to wait beyond fifteen weeks to have a procedure. Having more barriers to access, even ones we wish were helpful, contributes to later-term procedures, not to healthy family relationships.

TROUBLE IN NUMBERS

My friend Marion Banzhaf is the kind of feminist who wears an I HAD AN ABORTION T-shirt with TALK TO ME scrawled by hand beneath the message. Throughout the 1970s, she worked at feminist health centers, where she demonstrated vaginal self-exams and performed menstrual extractions. In its 1980s heyday, she was a pioneering member of the AIDS activist group ACT UP. She recounts the story of her abortion in a film I produced called *I Had an Abortion*.

The year was 1971, and there were only a couple of states, notably New York, where abortion was legal. Although her boyfriend thought they should drop out of school at the University of Florida and get married—they could live with his mother—Marion disagreed. She raised the money for her abortion in one afternoon by standing on the quad, asking for donations.

She then flew from Gainesville to New York, had her procedure, and, after she left the clinic, ran skipping down the street. "I was so happy to see that blood," she says, in a trademark Marion Banzhaf way (somewhat shocking, totally confident). "It meant I had my life back."

Dauntless radical though she is, there is one part of her abortion story she rarely tells. A year after her 1971 procedure, Marion got pregnant again. This time, she didn't have to worry about the money. Her new boyfriend pulled out his checkbook and put her on the next flight to New York City—and she knew it was the right decision. "But it was a much harder [abortion] for me personally. I felt I shouldn't let myself get pregnant," says Marion, now fifty-two. "Even to this day, I have shame about it. An accomplished, consciousness-raised feminist like me!"

One abortion, that happens. Two? Well, to paraphrase Oscar Wilde, two smacks of carelessness. My father, a doctor in Fargo, North Dakota, expressed surprise when I mentioned the second-abortion stigma to him: "It's odd, given that it's the exact same situation as before, no more or less of a life," he said. "It's as if women don't really believe they have the right to have abortions."

Dad, like Marion, is often shockingly logical. Still, abortion itself (whether your first or fourth) is so shrouded in secrecy, it's easy to imagine that only certain kinds of women would ever make a mistake like that twice. If "she" did, this almost unconscious thinking goes, it's clear "she" didn't care enough to learn from the first one. Fears about these repeat cases contribute to the unlovely idea that, because terminating a pregnancy is legal, women use abortion as birth control, leading to a cliché of this debate: the "I'm pro-choice, but I don't think it should be used as birth control" line.

In the clinic world, repeat visitors are called, not unkindly, "frequent fliers." The reason that casual term is not an insult is due simply to how common multiple abortions are. "You have three hundred possibilities to get pregnant in your life," says Peg Johnston, the director of an abortion clinic in Binghamton, New York. "A one percent failure rate—assuming the best possible use of contraception—is still three abortions," she says. "In what endeavor is a one percent failure rate not acceptable?"

According to Planned Parenthood, two out of every one hundred women aged fifteen to forty-four will have an abortion this year and half of them will have had at least one abortion previously. Yet virtually everyone I've talked to about multiple abortions said she shouldn't have let it happen again, implying it was her fault.

Why is that? Well, some of it is surely the anti-woman culture, a robust pro-life movement that, when abortion became legal, mobilized to scream at women on what is already not a fun day. But it's not just a vast right-wing conspiracy. Many women—pro-choice women—believe that abortion is taking a life (although not an independent life). What justifies that loss of life is the woman's own life. It's almost as if she is saying, "I recognize that this is serious, but my own life is too important to sacrifice for an unplanned pregnancy." But each additional abortion makes it harder to believe she is making an honorable decision.

Or that he is. My friend Matt, like many men in my life, has been part of more than one abortion. When he was younger, he was "knee-jerk pro-choice." If an unplanned pregnancy occurs in high school or college, he figured, of course you have an abortion. That's just common sense. He didn't revisit that with any sort of introspection until the first abortion, "But I wasn't in love with [the woman in question]. We had no future together. I was comfortable saying we needed to abort," Matt concludes. "I gave her money. She didn't express any need for me to be there with her."

He says, bluntly, that the second abortion felt "more like murder," and that he was disgusted at himself for being the reason his girl was at Planned Parenthood, confronting scary, toothless protesters and enduring this awful procedure. The circumstances had changed—Matt did have a future with the woman he got pregnant with the second time, although having a baby just then, a few months into their relationship, wasn't a good idea at all.

Mostly, though, it felt unseemly and immature to be there. "I sat at the clinic with all of these younger guys and I thought, *I am too old to be here, man,*" says Matt, now thirty-eight. "When do I stop giving myself the out? That is what abortion feels like— a free pass. But it's not totally free. There are emotional consequences, and as you get older, the sense of taking responsibility for your actions grows."

"There is something in that moment where you are supposed to smarten up," agrees Jenny Egan, a young ACLU staffer who had an abortion at age sixteen. "That is your one fuck-up. [After that] birth control can't fail and a condom can't break." But, as Jenny points out, the shame is often not the abortion itself—it's not the idea of killing a second baby when we are only allowed to kill one. The shame is the shame of getting pregnant. It means that you don't having enough control and power to take care of yourself.

Which brings us to a paradox of feminism. The success of the women's movement is not just in its overhaul of all of the institutions that kept women down—although it has made inroads in all of them, including national abortion rights, birth control for single people, and sexuality education (all under fire, and that last almost eradicated in favor of abstinence-only education). The more profound revolution, though, was the raised expectations this once-utopian movement suggested to its daughters. The mantra of empowerment means that women feel like responsible actors in sex—not merely ignorant victims—and that knowledge makes it harder, in a way, to justify the "mistake" of unplanned pregnancy. If you're so smart, if you read *Our Bodies, Ourselves* at age thirteen, if you knew about condoms, how did you get pregnant?

In *I Had an Abortion,* the film ends with dozens of women

saying, "My name is ____ and I had an abortion." A few—an older matron, a curly-haired professor type—admit, "I had two abortions." One woman says, "I had three abortions," and at a recent screening her presence provoked one young female audience member to wonder aloud why the multiple-abortion woman didn't use birth control and should we, the filmmakers, be promoting that?

At that same screening, a well-known Second Wave feminist, the writer Alix Kates Shulman, replied to the requisite "where's the birth control?" comment that she had had four abortions—"and not one was the result of carelessness." A few audience members vigorously nodded their heads in a "hear, hear" manner. But it looked as if most people quietly wondered if the birth control girl—the one pointing out that once is funny but twice is a spanking—was right.

In September of 2005, Pauline Bart, another Second Wave woman of some reputation within the movement, suggested at a screening of *I Had an Abortion* that younger women learn to do abortions themselves, just as the collective of women known as "Jane" did pre–*Roe v. Wade*.

"It's just like taking a melon baller and scooping out a melon," she said, referring to performing an abortion in one's own apartment. I nodded earnestly but thought, *No, it isn't.* Or at least it isn't to me. I don't doubt that some women experience abortion as devoid of angst, as Pauline Bart depicts, and for them each abortion is created equal.

For many women, though, getting pregnant when you don't want to be is because you made a mistake. Often the mistake is not your own fault—Alix was not told by her doctor that diaphragms could slip out of place; Marion got depressed on the high-dose pill and found it almost impossible to take. But if an abortion is meant to correct that mistake, is it anti-woman to presume a learning curve? I don't know. Fertility and sexuality are very complex. Let's be real: Some people are better at birth control than others. I've had unprotected sex more often than protected sex myself, so I'm hardly one to tsk-tsk.

Peg Johnston, the clinic director, thinks multiple abortions point to something larger than an individual snafu—occasionally that larger thing is carelessness, but usually in the context of a life out of control in other ways. Often it's a woman who has several children already and a chaotic, stressful life. At around $30 a month for the pill, others can't afford their birth control.

"That's very common," says Johnston, noting that a majority of the forty-five million uninsured in this country are women. Meanwhile, "some people are really fertile and others simply have lots and lots of sex. Frankly, if you have a lot of sex, you'll get pregnant more often."

As for Marion Banzhaf, she did find a way to make sure she didn't have another birth control failure but still had lots of sex. Soon after the second abortion, she came out as a lesbian.

—Originally published in *Nerve*, November 2005

MY BI-TRANS-FEMINIST POWER TRIP

December 25, 2010, I pull up at a Stop N Go in Fargo, North Dakota, to fill up my rental car. I'm catching a 6:00 AM flight the next day and don't trust that I'll be so organized at 4:00 AM with my two young sons in the car, a pitch-black sky, and the harsh tundra winds freezing my hands to the pump.

The checker at the counter is cute: a twentysomething wearing a loose black vest, button-down shirt, tie—a standard Stop N Go uniform, but on this River Phoenix lookalike, it looks stylish, I note approvingly. I feel a mildly flirtatious energy between us, one I often feel toward clerks, waiters, and bartenders whose job it is to be affable and bring me things for money. I accept my change and we exchange a second of genuine eye contact. *You're a pleasant surprise on this brutally cold day,* my eyes say. *I'm quietly confident and friendly,* the checker's eyes respond.

I push open the door and zip back to my car before the winds can whip through my coat and steal my body heat, thinking, *Man, things have changed in Fargo.* The checker was, I think, either a very butch young lesbian or a trans man, and I'd bet on the latter. I drive back to my parents' home pondering whether the vested checker chose to work on Christmas because his family didn't accept him, because he liked the overtime, or perhaps because he was Jewish—or all of the above.

A couple of decades earlier, there was another Stop N Go employee whom I also remember vividly. She was tall, with a carefully set hairdo and plastery pancake makeup. When I saw her, I'd feel an odd mixture of fascination and anxiety. Could it have been any more obvious that "she" was a man? I never ruminated about whether she had a family or wanted to work the late shift at Stop N Go. I assumed her life was tragic and lonely, like that of the Elephant Man. There was no meaningful eye contact with her; if anything, I labored to be neutral when I was so clearly uncomfortable, almost hysterical, in her presence. I'm amazed now at how easy it was for me to objectify the trans woman in 1985, especially given how easy it was to flirt with the trans man and see him as a human being today. I can't help but assume that not only have I changed, but the world has, too.

Indeed it has. Since Sigmund Freud asserted at the turn of the twentieth century that all humans have a capacity for bisexuality, and a male and female side (purloining the latter insight from his own guy crush, Wilhelm Fliess), society has been dealing consciously with an invitation not just to understand complicated attractions to others, but to explore the complex role of gender within ourselves. When Alfred Kinsey created his famous Kinsey scale, he cast sexuality as a continuum. Being able to see sexuality as not just straight (i.e., normal) and its opposite, gay (abnormal), primed people to understand that gender, too, might be distributed across a spectrum. Thus, comprehending sexuality—bisexuality—lends itself to understanding transgenderism. The two are inextricably linked—and not just as the most recent initials in the LGBT label.

The movement for queer civil and human rights is a crucial ascendant fight right now, animated by the same urgency and backlash directed at feminists and African Americans decades ago. The benefits of this movement are easily found. In 1990, there were two Gay-Straight Alliances in the country; by 2010, there were more than four thousand GSAs in schools across the country. In 2011, same-sex marriage is available in a handful of states; a decade ago, that number was zero. There are now summer camps for children who identify themselves as another gender—and there is enough consciousness of transgenderism that a ten-year-old can tell his parents he was born in a girl's body but is a boy, and know that he is not abnormal and is far from alone.

I WAS A beneficiary of gaystreaming—the mainstreaming of gay rights. When I fell in love, at twenty-two, with a fellow female intern at *Ms.* magazine and had to think about queer politics and feminism in a much more practical way, I didn't feel alone or that my life was somehow lawful. There were problems, however. I was immediately perceived as a lesbian—poof! Overnight, all of my previous dating experience was rendered false. A couple years later, I began dating a petite and fey man and was immediately recategorized as "actually straight." A year later, I fell in with a woman again (albeit a very masculine one) and there you had it: Instantly gay!

As perceptions of me ping-ponged back and forth, I felt most myself as both gay and straight—or neither—and became bolder about declaring who I was: bisexual. I sort of disliked the label, but couldn't think of anything better. I called myself bisexual because, as activist Robyn Ochs always says, "I acknowledge that I have the potential to be attracted to more than one gender or sex, but not necessarily to the same degree or at the same time." Still, I feel awkward at times offering the term to describe myself—as if I am hell-bent on answering a personal question that no one has really asked me.

"The word *bisexual* may not be perfect," wrote Julia Serano in 2010, referring to how it is often inaccurately maligned as "reinforcing the binary"—the binary being the feminist equivalent of bedbugs. "But it does have a rich political history, one that involves fighting for visibility and inclusion both within and outside of the queer community."

Robyn Ochs calls herself a survivor of the bad times in the lesbian and gay movements, before people could tell the truth about being bisexual and transgendered. She helped to organize bisexual women and men in Massachusetts, and it isn't a coincidence that the state with the most active bisexual organizations was also the first to legalize gay marriage and other protections for queer people. The entitlement that bisexual people were accused of having—straight privilege—was also their secret weapon. They believed they deserved full human rights, because they had enjoyed them when in an opposite-sex relationship.

I've thought about that rich political history a lot over the years, especially as bisexuality continues to be disbelieved and demeaned by many straight and gay people, and remains largely invisible in the culture as anything other than a titillating sweeps-week gambit. Bisexuality is still somewhat invisible within the queer rights movement because it is visible only in certain situations—when one is polyamorous or single. Our continuing invisibility links us to trans people in general and trans feminists in particular. Transgendered people are also disbelieved, believed to be a fake woman or man.

DURING THE FIRST leg of book touring with my first book, *Manifesta* (a manifesto about current feminism, coauthored with Amy Richards) in 2000, two trans women attended a reading in Portland, Oregon. We were at In Other Words, a feminist bookstore, a space I felt was created for me and mine. The women were Emi and Diana, two well-known feminist activists. I had met Diana years earlier, at a Riot Grrrl–esque feminist conference called Foxfire in Olympia, Washington, at which she performed a spontaneous striptease to demystify a trans female body that hadn't been surgically reassigned. She also spoke at the anti-violence rally that evening about her experience in an abusive relationship and about the lack of resources for trans women, who were often turned away at shelters for having a penis. I thought she seemed like she needed a lot of attention.

Both Emi and Diana wanted to know why *Manifesta* didn't address trans experience. My internal reaction was: *Why are you two men here in this women-only place, taking up so much space and critiquing me? You have male privilege. You know how I can tell? Because you feel like you can waltz into a women-only space and take over!*

I now recognize my reaction as bigoted, a function of ignorance and feeling threatened by something I didn't understand, mixed with the embarrassment of being called out in this setting.

At first blush, trans people have the opposite problem bisexuals do: If anything, they are too visible, as evidenced by my extremely vivid memory of the trans woman who worked at Stop N Go in the 1980s. It's part of the current human condition to notice gender right away; most of us feel an urgent need to sort people into male or female. But transgendered people in fact suffer from a similar kind of belittling assumption—that one's external genitalia denote gender. But transpeople disagree; they say that what we *see* as their gender doesn't trump or undermine what each individual *feels* is his or her gender. Thus, gender is conferred not by penis or vagina (at least not solely), but by a deeply personal, interior, and psychological sense of what one's gender is.

While there are no good statistics about the prevalence of transgendered people, we know that about .25 to 1 percent of the population identifies as transsexual to statisticians, and this number doesn't include gender-variant or gender-queer people. Still, this relatively low percentage translates into hundreds of thousands of people. The broader social acceptance is reflected in how many younger people identify as trans, and the anecdotal evidence will, I hope, be followed eventually by better statistics. These are things I've learned since that day more than a decade ago when I met Emi and Diana.

Back then, I did feel extremely self-righteous about two things: I was confident that Emi and Diana were manifesting privilege, and I was confident that privilege was bad. Soon after, this ironclad denunciation of having any unearned advantage felt contradictory to me. After all, I finally got over my guilt about straight privilege in certain settings, and I had a revelation about bisexuality that struck me as deeply feminist. There is a fundamental error in how bisexuality is understood. It's perceived as being conferred by your partner. But (and here's the revelation) your sexuality isn't bequeathed to you; it comes from you. Thus, bisexuals aren't confused or broken, but a culture that tells us we are is broken and must be changed. This is vintage personal-is-political feminist theory.

I applied that feminist lens to my life and began seeing myself as having some human rights as a bisexual woman. I had the right to self-identify, not to be told who I was. I had the right to have acknowledgment, compassion, and interest from friends and loved ones about my relationship, regardless of the gender of my partner. I had the right and the responsibility to make friends with my privilege.

In thinking more about my own privilege, I began to see how shortsighted it was to merely critique it as a corrupt influence. Wasn't privilege—access to higher education, health insurance, marriage for those who seek it, as well as dignity and respect—what we in social justice movements were fighting for, but for all people? What were the concrete aspects of male privilege that I felt transwomen benefited from, anyway? In the case of Emi and Diana at In Other Words, I perceived their ability to advocate forcefully on their own behalf as a product of their having been raised with male privilege. Their presence, however, challenged me to ask why I didn't feel I could be just as aggressive myself. I decided to try to grab some of that privilege (that is, take up space), rather than ask Emi and Diana to make themselves more meek.

As I began to make friends with my own privilege, I had to confront the options for what conscious, feminist people do with privilege. These options fall into three categories: denial, guilt, and positive force. Denial is categorically bad. Guilt is a natural reaction and even a step toward dealing with privilege, but it's not constructive—and holding on to it is another form of privilege and indulgence. Positive force means that we can use our power in the service of activism and social justice. Rather than be ashamed that I got married when same-sex couples still could not in forty-four states, I could direct guests to give money to marriage-equality campaigns in lieu of toasters and Nambé salt and pepper shakers. I could use my entitlement to aid the visibility of gay people, as couples with a trans partner could when they married. I could focus on the work yet to do by having conversations with loved ones, not just lawmakers.

AFTER YEARS OF working in feminism, I've had to rethink all of the assumptions I entered the movement believing. I'm ashamed that I was once so bigoted with regard to transpeople, but I'm proud that I evolved—as feminism and feminists must—when faced with new information and new times. I wonder sometimes about that cute guy at the Stop N Go. Was the nice vibe I felt between the two of us due to progress? Mostly, I ponder how our chance meeting framed both of our places on the continuum of sexuality and gender, underscoring all that feminism has done to liberate individuals to be whoever they are.

Bisexual and transgendered people continue to nudge queer and straight and cisgendered communities into a deeper understanding of being human—and that is our particular, and spectacular, contribution to the movement.

Q&A

Julia Serano

I KNOW IN MY BONES THAT MISOGYNY EXISTS, BUT SOME-
times it's hard for me to put my finger on the ways in which our culture
still clearly demeans women. That's why Julia Serano and her 2007 book,
*Whipping Girl: A Transsexual Woman on Sexism and the Scapegoating of
Femininity,* are so crucial. Using the frame of transgenderism, she demonstrates that our culture says, "Men—yeah, men! Who wouldn't want to
be a man? Men are *great!"* which can bolster trans masculine people. By
contrast, trans women or people on the feminine spectrum are perceived
as inferior and more questionable and are treated as entertainers and
sex objects.

Julia, a forty-three-year-old evolutionary biologist originally from
Philly, is a trans woman, writer, activist, and spoken-word artist. She offers
readers an almost scientific comparison, experienced in the laboratory of
her life, of how men are treated versus women. Julia is brilliant, friendly,
and fetching—a tomboyish, bisexual Bay Area lady with bangs and pink
Chuck Taylors. When I read how her transgender experience was defined

 by traditional sexism, I saw good old-fashioned misogyny anew—and felt its unfairness in a way I hadn't since I was twenty and reading *Backlash* for the first time.

Jennifer: What was your family like?

Julia: Basically, I am half Italian American and half Irish American. Dad is a stockbroker; Mom was a homemaker. I was the oldest of five children, although one of my sisters died of SIDS, so there were four of us growing up. All girls. I initially appeared to be the exception to that, but I eventually proved them wrong.

JB: Were you always a feminist?

JS: To some extent, but not nearly as much as after I transitioned. Because I was moving through the world as male, I wasn't sure I could call myself feminist. I thought of myself more as a feminist ally before then. Also, I had a blind spot in regard to misogyny. I experienced some of it because I was a pretty effeminate guy before I transitioned. I didn't think of that as misogyny, I thought of that as homophobia. Numerous of my former partners, including my partner who I was with when I transitioned, were outspoken feminists and told me to research feminism. After I transitioned, it became very obvious to me, the ways in which I experienced misogyny.

JB: What are some of the distinctions between the ways you experienced misogyny as a trans woman versus what you were hearing about from your partner, from a cisgendered woman?

JS: When I think about experiencing misogyny, there are two different contexts. There's the context of everyday life, where I move through the world and people don't necessarily know that I'm trans, so I experience misogyny like most cis women do. Then there are experiences where people know I'm a trans woman—that's a little bit different. I had heard a lot about misogyny and what women experienced, so whether it's walking down the street and men running up to talk to you, or catcalls, or being in a situation where men talk over you or treat you in a particular way, these are things I'd heard about before, but the experience of having that happen to me firsthand was very visceral and evoked a lot of feelings of frustration and anger and annoyance. I would say that those experiences are not that different [from cis women's], but I had the experience of moving through the world as male beforehand, and then being thrust into it, rather than experiencing it on different levels my whole life.

I talk about "transmisogyny" in my book, which is the intersection of being trans and experiencing misogyny. As a trans woman, I don't just experience how our culture devalues femininity—I'm treated as a fake woman. I find that men who know I'm trans will be abruptly forward, thinking that trans women are more sexual. Then there's a tendency within queer communities for trans men to be more respected and perceived as less frivolous than trans women. Trans women tend to be seen as drag artists— just there for entertainment.

JB: How do you think transgenderism has impacted feminism, especially recently? I feel like I've seen such an enormous change. Younger feminists seem to question gender almost automatically, whether or not they would ever identify as trans themselves, and seem to get energy from the idea of gender being more fluid, in a way that feminists fifteen years ago did not.

JS: In the last five years, I've observed an acceptance of trans people and an acknowledgment that transgender people's experiences fall within the realm of feminism's concerns. Within younger circles, there's kind of an appropriating of trans, in that it's discussed in terms of challenging the gender binary, but there's less concern about the actual issues that transgender people face.

For example, people might be interested in my experiences as a trans woman, in my experiences with misogyny, or about how I defy gender norms, but when we get to the issue of how sometimes trans women, because of their anatomy, are put into all-male jail cells, or if we get into issues of trans people actually surviving in the world and the issues that they face, there is less interest about that.

JB: It's more of an abstract, intellectual, ruminating interest, as opposed to a real, concrete, activism interest?

JS: Yes. It's definitely an abstract interest, rather than being concerned about activism that's being done in order to help transpeople be able to move through the world safely. Within academic settings, and within certain feminist activist circles, there's more of a tendency for cisgender feminists to relate to transmen's experiences than to transwomen's experiences. I think there are a lot of reasons for this: Part of it is just by being assigned as female from birth—there are a lot of similarities there—and I think a lot of cisgender feminists who kind of feel that they've been put into this box of *female* can kind of relate to people in the trans masculine spectrum a lot more easily. And I think that there is the reality that a lot of people on the trans masculine spectrum are involved in feminist circles, are women's studies majors, are gender studies majors, before their transitions, so I think there's more of an ease of allowing trans masculine people into feminism.

On a real-life, logistical level, there's not nearly that level of acceptance for people on the trans feminine spectrum within feminist settings. For example, I spent my entire early adulthood as male and feeling I was a feminist ally, but not actually feeling like I could actually call myself a feminist or get really involved. It's really hard, I think, for those of us who are trans women to bridge that gap. Because of that, I think that transfeminine-spectrum people have had less of an impact on feminism than transmasculine-spectrum people, which is something I'm hoping, as time goes on, will change more.

JB: Trans men do seem to walk more freely within feminism, just as men walk more freely in the broader culture. For instance, trans men have attended Michigan during periods when trans women couldn't do so openly. When you lived as a man, was there really any reason to see yourself as not fully a feminist? I don't want people to think they can't call themselves feminist based on their genitals or how they were raised.

JS: I hear you. I think the environment has changed, partially because of increased acceptance of trans issues. Looking back fifteen years ago, even LGB kinds of issues were seen as more separate from feminism than they are now. Now, it's definitely easier for men, whether trans men or cis men, to become actively involved in feminism. Trans people and queer-people issues are being seen as feminist issues. I definitely think that men can and should be feminists.

Many cisgender feminists find this controversial to say, but men's gender expressions are really highly policed in our culture. That's not to take away from the fact that femininity is often put under a microscope and women are judged more on their appearance than men are. Still, men have far less leeway to experiment with gender than women in our culture. I think there's a lot more recognition of this among cisgender men. A lot of those issues are related to misogyny. I think that cisgender men recognize these issues more, and there's room for them to be involved in feminism—and for feminism to be concerned with the range of gendered experiences people have.

JB: When I wrote *Look Both Ways*, it emanated from my own experience thinking about how girls could fall in love with a friend and

have a space for that not to be labeled. A lot of men would come to the readings and say, "Why didn't you include men in this book? Do you think there's differences in how women and men are treated regarding sexuality?"

The differences are huge! One of the nice elements of being female and oppressed is that no one really takes what you do in bed seriously. Girls' fooling around together is perceived as a lark and sort of pointless, whereas guys' fooling around is seen as actual sex and a big deal and therefore punished.

JS: True. If there's not a penis involved, no sex is happening. [*Laughs.*]

JB: **Being bisexual and a cis woman made me understand invisibility has freedom, too. I definitely got to fumble and figure things out, and it wasn't policed, as you say.**

JS: I've had conversations with my transgender female friends where someone will say, "How can we possibly say that men's genders are policed more than women's genders?" So I'll tell them little anecdotes from my experiences before I transitioned. For example, at one point I had a red umbrella. It's the Bay Area. It's always raining in winter, so I was always carrying my red umbrella. I can't tell you how many people commented negatively on the fact that I had a red umbrella. "Oh, is that your girlfriend's umbrella? Are you borrowing her umbrella?" Something as little and silly as having a red umbrella made me suspect.

JB: **I never thought of umbrellas as being gendered like that. But it's not just that men are really tightly policed whenever they color outside the lines. It's also that it's then perceived as being somehow feminine, which is then hated.**

JS: Definitely. Even the fact that ten years ago in our society, we had to create a new word—"metrosexual"—to describe men who actually cared about their appearance.

JB: Both my sons have long hair, and they're often perceived as girls. People will ask their names and hear Skyler and Agnes, instead of Skuli and Magnus. When I say, "Actually, he's a boy," they respond, "Oh! I'm sorry!" They're jarred by having made a mistake and also freaked out by the fact that they think this male child is presenting as female. It's like our culture is in an awkward stage. People who five years from now will be knowledgeable about, comfortable with, and familiar with trans issues are right now at a point where they don't have an investment in being bigots but they're far from being allies. They resent having to negotiate new language and terminology, like "cisgender" versus "trans," and new pronouns, like "zee," "hir," and the singular "they."

JS: Trans is where lesbian and gay culture was in the late '80s and early '90s. You can watch TV and see transgender characters; they're usually pretty horrific, but at least they're not only serial killers, right? Sometimes they're characters you're supposed to like, even though a lot of the jokes are kind of about the transperson. There are still regions of the country where I could go that people would absolutely freak out if they knew who I was. At the same time, I live in the Bay Area, where people at my work know that I'm trans, and the people here in my life, rather than being dismissive, want to be supportive and accepting—even if they occasionally do things that bother me.

You have to meet people where they are. Someone who thinks that transgender people are monsters and predators isn't ready to learn the word "cisgender." If you're in a more progressive area, like a city, or you're on a college campus, then people have even more awareness. If you're involved in progressive or feminist or queer politics, then a lot of times you find people who are not just onboard but are righteous allies.

JB: What defines a "righteous ally"?

JS: A righteous ally is someone who has schooled themselves on the issues trans people face and the ways in which we're marginalized. I don't have to go out of my way to explain my situation to them. They know what "trans woman" means. They might already describe themselves as cisgender. They don't slip up with their pronouns. People who are accepting and trying to be supportive sometimes say things that kind of imply that I'm not really as much of a woman, or a real woman, even if they don't realize their language is like that. Allies know better and teach the people in their life about other people's issues. If I'm not around and a friend of theirs makes a joke about trans people, an ally would say, "Hey, that joke is kind of fucked up, and this is why." Those two aspects—schooling oneself and others—can be applied to being an ally of any movement.

JB: How do you define feminism?

JS: I see feminism as a movement to challenge all forms of sexism, and I would define sexism as any kind of double standard that's applied based on gender or sexuality.

JB: I like that! People usually go to the dictionary definition—points for original thinking!

JS: People most often think of feminism as a women's movement—a women's rights or women's issues movement. That's true, but I am of the frame of mind that there are lots of different forms of sexism and they're all interrelated. They're all about policing and limiting people based on gender.

JB: "People policing other people's genders"—it's so clear what you mean. I can't stand the term "gender binary" anymore. It's jargon inserted in place of actually saying something descriptive and understandable.

JS: Right, and if we say that the gender binary is bad, then we put ourselves in the position of criticizing people because they're "reinforcing the gender binary"—appearing feminine or masculine—and that's just another way of policing people's sexuality. I'm opposed.

—Interviewed on January 19, 2011

LESBIAN AFTER MARRIAGE

Deborah Abbott was somewhat happily married to a nice man with whom she'd created two adorable sons before she realized that the intense rapport she felt with her best friend, Rachel, was the first step toward love and "unbelievably thrilling" sex with women. After separating from her husband, she'd often laugh at her dueling identities. "I would be at the PTA meeting and people would assume that I was heterosexual," says Abbott. "And then I'd be dancing at a club and people would be shocked to learn I had an ex-husband and kids!"

Abbott can giggle now, but when she began looking for resources for "married lesbians" back in the early 1980s, she found nothing and felt lonely. So she started her own support group in Santa Cruz, California, called "From Wedded Wife to Lesbian Life," which would also become the name of her 1995 book published by Crossing Press. "I have women who've come for years," says Abbott, currently the director of the Gay, Lesbian, Bisexual, and Transgender Resource Center at the University of California, Santa Cruz. "We are a community." And the newbies? "They look around the room and weep with relief," she adds. "They say, 'Everyone looks so normal!'"

Abbott's group sees about one hundred women a year who pretty much thought they were straight through years of marriage and child rearing, only to have a change of heart later in life. Call them LAMs—or lesbians after marriage: These are the women who have tied the knot, procreated, and, once the children are out of the home or more independent, found love in the arms of a woman.

The first mom of my acquaintance to go on the LAM was my high school voice teacher, a fascinating and dramatic lady with three daughters and a husband who had taught me to sing "Macavity" at the top of my lungs. I admit I was shocked when I heard the rumor that she had left town and was involved with a lady musician. Then my college roommate told me that her mother (two kids, twenty years of heterosexual marriage) was getting hitched in Hawaii to a woman. More recently, my good friend's sixty-year-old mother phoned her to report she is in the midst of a white-hot lesbian affair, having never mentioned or acted on any Sapphic attraction before in her life. Conversations and similar tallies with other friends confirmed the trend: LAMs are the new LUGs (lesbians until graduation).

LAM sounds like a joke, especially given the derision directed at LUGs—the phenomenon of young women who never thought they were gay yet find themselves madly in love with a girl, usually while at college. In part because of their youth (and in part because of misogyny), it's assumed that these young women's actions are contrived, designed merely to better attract a *Girls Gone Wild*–consuming heterosexual male. LUGs are common and yet tragically misunderstood. According to writer (and LUG) Laura Eldridge, coauthor of *The No-Nonsense Guide to Menopause,* people usually identify college as the time when biology yields to social and cultural pressure, but it is probably more true that it's the other way around. "The perception is that the college campus environment encourages straight girls to engage in lesbian behavior in the same way it might lead you to be an ardent communist for a couple years or get an ill-advised tattoo," says Eldridge. "Then, the belief goes, you stop all these games, admit who you truly are, and find a man."

That's backward, says Eldridge. In fact, "social pressures on women to marry and have children really start to kick in during your twenties." So in your coed days you're free to fall for women if you have the inclination; as you get closer to the childbearing end date, that social freedom constricts. Eldridge thinks that many bisexual women start to focus on dating men "not because they were pretending same-sex desire *before* but because they are giving in to intense social expectations now."

A growing body of research on women's sexuality indicates that Eldridge may be right. "LUGs have always existed in some form, but the difference is context," says Lisa Diamond, a psychology professor at the University of Utah and the author of a book from Harvard University Press called *Sexual Fluidity: Understanding Women's Love and Desire.* "College is the first time a lot of women have been given the space to even ask themselves the questions *Who do I desire?* or *What do I want?*" This is different from twenty or thirty years ago, says Diamond, when college served as a backdrop in the mad rush to find a husband. Everyone from "Compulsory Heterosexuality and Lesbian Existence" author Adrienne Rich to novelist Alix Kates Shulman has attested that back then *everything* was about getting a man to the altar. Going to college, working—it all led inexorably to wifedom. Perhaps just as many women were attracted to both men and women in those days, but they tended "to be married already," says Diamond, and didn't know how to act on this fluidity.

Nor did they have the time. "When one's children are young, finding the ideal companion is not your first priority," says therapist, writer, and former LAM Amy Bloom. "You're just trying to keep up with your responsibilities." Women didn't ask themselves, *What do I want?* until they had a few kids, glimpsed their first copy of *Ms.* magazine, and realized there might be more to life after all.

There's more than just social pressures acting on our libidos; there's the call of the wild, the evolutionary compulsion to procreate. "I do remember kind of a biological *grrr*—a craving for intercourse—that really picked up with some serious speed at age twenty-eight," says Anastasia Higginbotham, a Brooklyn-based writer who primarily had girlfriends from age twenty to twenty-nine, one of whom was me (age twenty-three to twenty-five, in case you're wondering). "My fantasies shifted—that's where I really noticed it. All of my sexual fantasies suddenly involved penetration or men, and they had never, *never* been that way before." Higginbotham also recalls that her ovulation cycles were stronger, and "when I was ovulating it was like I was in heat, so it was hard to be in a relationship with my girlfriend, who was so not going through the same thing."

Perhaps it's no coincidence that women choose women when they are most decidedly trying not to get pregnant—teens, early twenties, after having a few kids—and [choose] men when they are most in touch with their biological clock. Consider these well-documented same-sex "defections" among younger women: Rebecca Walker (who recently broke up with longtime girlfriend Meshell Ndegeocello and had a baby with a man), Ani DiFranco (who married a man in her late twenties and recently had a baby with her current man), and the inimitable Anne Heche, who left Ellen DeGeneres and married cameraman Coley Laffoon not a year after their breakup. Baby Homer came one year after that. Of course, in Heche's case, the divorce came not long after the baby—and another baby with a new guy—but so it goes with many LAMs.

DISCARDED LABELS

The stories in *From Wedded Wife to Lesbian Life* speak not just to a newfound and profound desire for women but to the resentment that unequal gender status breeds, particularly after marriage. Witness this dispatch from Robin Finley, who lived harmoniously with a man for four years and then made the mistake of marrying him: "Before [the marriage] we had the utmost idealism about our relationship and discussed every little decision in detail," she writes. "With marriage, assumptions became the rule, and blatant sexism reared its head: If I worked late, I was a workaholic. If he worked late, he was just meeting the demands of his job." In the same book, well-known activist JoAnn Loulan, who wrote the books *Lesbian Sex, The Lesbian Erotic Dance,* and *Lesbian Passion,* was asked to compare lesbian "marriage" to heterosexual marriage. "As a lesbian I don't feel any concerns about the power differential whatsoever. I absolutely hold my own, power-wise," Loulan wrote. "There's this freedom in lesbianism in that I'm not seen as a role. I am not a wife. So, therefore, I don't have to 'do anything.' I don't have to cook. I don't have to clean. I don't have to be the one to take care of the kids."

But caretaking that's oppressive when one-sided can be utterly gratifying when it's returned and free-flowing, as it often is among women. Brooklyn-based writer and teacher Sara Jane Stoner (once bisexual, now full-on "queer") has watched her gorgeous "trophy wife" mother ("she's budget-trophy—she shops at TJ Maxx") nurse four of her friends through cancer, one of whom died. "While the husbands in these situations begin to travel—constantly," says Stoner, "my mother is there vacuuming up her friends' dead skin cells after chemo. She does the care." Stoner admits to having fantasies of her mom going on the LAM.

While a desperate housewife who gets her emotional needs

met by her lady friends isn't quite a lesbian, she might be one down the road, given the sexual flexibility that is increasingly viewed as the norm for women. A LAM, just like a five-star lesbian, might find herself attracted to men if in the right situation. "There is now a lot of good, nationally representative data indicating that a majority of women who are attracted to women are also attracted to men," says Diamond, who for years has conducted her own ongoing study of sexual-minority women. "Many of the die-hard lesbians in my study found that they were attracted to men if they were in a position around lots of men." For instance, one longtime lesbian Diamond interviewed became very close friends with a male student at graduate school and finally fell in love with him and even got married. She believed she was still exclusively attracted to women, except for her husband, but avoided giving her sexuality any labels, saying, "I feel like I'm a lesbian who happened to fall in love with this one guy, and people don't accept that."

Because she's married, people just assume she's an average heterosexual, says Diamond, "so she makes a point of telling folks that she's bisexual. She realizes that saying 'lesbian who's with a man' will not really fly, so she settles for 'bisexual' so that they won't assume she's heterosexual."

Diamond cites this example as evidence that women's sexual fluidity is not based primarily on avoiding the stigma of being gay. "It's the opposite: Now that she's with a man, she makes efforts not to just slip into 'heterosexual privilege,'" says Diamond, "and in fact to 'spoil' that privilege by informing people that although she's married, she's not straight."

LAMs tend not to identify as bisexual but to see their current state as permanent, though many eventually re-partner with men. LAMs Amy Bloom and JoAnn Loulan are now with men; older lesbians such as Alice Walker, Jan Clausen (who wrote the memoir

Apples and Oranges about this transition), and women's music star Holly Near are in love relationships with men. "We talk a lot about not worrying about labels," says Abbott of the philosophy in her support group. "I say, focus on how you are feeling right now, what draws you right now." In other words, ask that radical question: *What do you want?*

—Originally published in *Out,* October 2007

BI FOR NOW

"The other night, I met a girl that reminded me of you," my friend Elizabeth said. It was a steamy Saturday afternoon last May, and I was rushing down a narrow Greenwich Village street to buy flowers for my wedding. "This girl, she was smart and feminist and said she was bisexual," Elizabeth continued. "I told her about you, and I said, 'I know how this works. You'll be married in ten years.'"

It's hard when your wedding day is used as evidence that your life is a sham.

On a certain level, though, I understand the confusion. How can you be bisexual and married? If marriage isn't about picking a team, what is?

My wedding day run-in with Elizabeth made me think. I never thought I'd marry, even before I fell in love with a female intern at my first magazine job in New York. That relationship—surprising, shocking, and thrilling all at once—jolted my identity. I had been a straight Midwestern gal; a bisexual city dweller began to emerge.

MY TWENTIES AND thirties were a series of big loves with men and women, but the biggest one of all was Amy. She was an electrifying, alluringly butch musician who also happened to be one half of the Indigo Girls. She had a Georgia accent, a kind soul, and such selfless politics, she made Jimmy Carter looked like Graydon Carter. We met in Montana when I flew out to cover a series of concerts the Indigo Girls were doing to support Native American environmental activists. It was love and lust at first sight, spurring me to break up with my boyfriend and confirming the fact that I was not a straight girl. Soon we were flying back and forth between Atlanta and New York City, meeting on the road during her long tours, and spending holidays with each other's families. Her friends were attractive, progressive lesbians and inspiring musicians; mine were New York writers and feminists. I loved being in her world and she embraced mine.

I never wanted to marry Amy, but the fact that I couldn't in most states made weddings attended with her poignant, vaguely itchy affairs—the celebration of heterosexual legal commitment was alienating. A friend once asked me if Amy and I were going to get hitched and I felt a surge of gratitude that almost made me cry—not because I had my dress all picked out, but because someone at least saw our wedding as an option. It's difficult to reject something that has rejected you first.

Some of my resistance to marriage was driven by my feminist politics. I was keenly attuned to the compromises associated with being a wife—from being the helper, rather than the main event, to the endless unpaid tedious labor. "Why I Want a Wife," an essay in an early issue of *Ms.* magazine (always on my mother's coffee table) had a profound effect on my thinking at a young age. Poet Jan Clausen's line "If I'm going to be a wife, I damn well get to have one, too," was something I quoted approvingly. My five-year relationship with Amy was co-wifely: loving, healthy, and egalitarian. We discussed politics, hiked on the Appalachian Trail, hung out with our families, and supported each other's work. We recycled, cooked together, rescued kittens, traveled to Cuba and all over the United States, and found lots and lots of time for sex. For once, orgasms were easy. I was amazed by how vulnerable I could be in bed with her.

By contrast, my relationships with men always left me feeling somewhat hopeless, like a clichéd version of myself—naggy, competitive, and quick to complain about how "emotionally unavailable" he was. I held something in reserve with men and I was dismissive of "typical couples," with their public bickering and soothing of fragile male egos. I despaired of finding the kind of relationship I wanted with a guy and, because of my ability to fall in love with women, I didn't try too hard. Men had their charms (lustful assertiveness, an air of mystery, fun body parts), but I had to acknowledge that my better self—the more confident, funny, fully Jenny Jennifer—came out with only one gender.

In 2002, Amy and I broke up. Traveling so much had gone from glamorous to onerous, and neither of us was willing to give up her home to live in the other's city. I was feeling curious about men, too, and increasingly returned the flirtation of a sexy and misanthropic musician/public school teacher named Gordon. In part to shield myself from the fear and sadness I felt about leaving Amy, I threw myself into this new relationship. Within weeks I was making excuses to my friends about his rudeness and saying things like, "You just don't get his sense of humor. He's actually *hilarious.*" I swung between hating him and hating myself. Occasionally I hated both of us, but it was impossible to love us both at the same time. In a moment of self-respect, I broke up with him. In an ensuing moment of denial, we got pregnant. I had a baby, Skuli, but aborted the relationship with Gordon. I focused on my son, and romance slid off my radar and settled in a remote corner of my to-do list ("item #121: procure love life").

The first three years of my son's life were full with writing, book tours, friends, family, and the seemingly endless dramedies of the little boy with whom I lived. I was single for the first time in my adult life, and it felt surprisingly great. My whole romantic life had been reacting to things: I feared subsuming my ambitions under a man's, so I partnered with women; I grew frustrated with the symbiosis I felt with Amy and threw myself into someone who was her (and my) opposite. I didn't want to get married just because I was pregnant, it's the most culturally acceptable, or my spouse wanted me to, so I took marriage off the menu. Being alone with Skuli felt very luxurious. Sometimes I would wake up in the dead of night, Skuli's little form snuggled next to me, and think, *Life is really good.* But, delectable as it was, at thirty-seven, I sensed I was too young to have Skuli be my bedmate for eternity. I decided to put my love life on the top of my to-do list.

I dated men only this time around. It's hard to know why, but my sexuality isn't some equal opportunity employer, it has its own logic and serendipity. Just as I was starting to feel like I had my mojo back, I ran into Michael, an old friend of my sister's, on a subway platform. He was broad-shouldered, big-eyed, and tall, his hair a thatch of floppy blondness. We exchanged pleasantries and as I was leaving, I squeezed his arm and said that I hoped our paths would cross again. That night, I Facebooked Michael. We agreed to meet for a drink later that week. When Michael arrived, he handed me a bag of chocolate chip cookies from a nearby bakery. "These are for Skuli," he said, pronouncing my son's odd Icelandic name perfectly. It was as if there was a bible for how to properly date a single mother and not only had Michael read it, he'd written it.

His single-mother handling skills were one thing, but he understood me as someone who can love women and men, and didn't reduce my relationships to phases. Like many men of his age, he has dated bisexual women. He's proudly supportive of my career as a feminist writer and activist, dedicated to making my chaotic life easier, and makes me, an exhausted mother of two, feel like the sexiest woman in the world.

Although Michael wanted to get married, he accepted that I didn't and left it at that. Soon, we were pregnant and living together, and an insta-family of (almost) four. That's when I took a breath and realized I kind of wanted to marry *him*. I had a child with someone else; I wanted something with Michael I hadn't had with anyone. On the one-year anniversary of our first date, a little tipsy after dinner at Hearth, I proposed. Eight months later, in front of our parents, siblings, nieces and nephews, and our own children, we said, "I do." My family was surprised and thrilled, but no one, thank God, acted relieved.

My lifelong mate is male, but it didn't change my sexuality. I believe that my sexuality is something that emanates from me—not something conferred on me by my partner. On the other hand, I'm aware I appear straight, because bisexuality is invisible (or unbelievable) to many people. I know I'm not straight and never will be. I'm really proud of who I am and I'm lucky that Michael is, too.

If I had to pick the first moment I knew it might be safe, even wonderful, to be Michael's wife, it was on our third date. "You're the best boyfriend—or girlfriend—I have ever had," I blurted. Michael paused. Then, in a way I knew meant he got it and me, he said, "*Thank* you."

At our wedding, I forgot the bouquet I had run out to buy hours earlier. We fashioned a makeshift arrangement out of some flowers on the table. When I married Michael, I didn't feel like I picked a team—but I do feel like I'm part of one.

—Originally published in *Harper's Bazaar*, May 2011

Q&A

Amy Ray

I REMEMBER VERY CLEARLY THE FIRST TIME I SAW AMY.

It was 1988, and the Indigo Girls' video for "Closer to Fine" was on the big-screen TV at the Lawrence University union. The Atlanta duo looked exciting and different to me. What was it? The sincere and direct gaze, the thin lips, seeing two women who could play guitar, walk, and sing at the same time? They weren't chicks or eye candy; they seemed to occupy the same serious space as male musicians.

For a long time in my life, I couldn't imagine someone who embodied what I thought an ideal feminist woman was more than Amy Ray, the throaty brunette Indigo Girl. She was strong, not only physically, but also as a presence. You noticed her for having substance: a deep, charmingly scratchy voice with something to say; large, watchful green eyes that signaled interest in and engagement with the world. There was nothing furtive or dodgy about Amy.

Elizabeth Wurtzel once wrote of her as embodying the female gaze, to counter the objectifying, flattening male gaze. She didn't bother with

makeup or skirts, yet she always looked alluring. Amy also had power I had most often associated with men. She earned her own considerable wealth, played guitar, and wrote loud, beseeching music. And she was deeply, unapologetically political—never ate anything that had a face, lived frugally, gave generously, and felt most at home with Native American environmentalists, Zapatistas, and queer kids. Two decades after I first laid eyes on her, she still embodies feminism to me, mainly because she struggles so valiantly to match her words to her actions.

Jennifer: What was it like for you growing up?

Amy: I had conservative parents, but they had an interesting relationship to feminism. Until puberty, they treated us pretty much as genderless, aside from sticking us in dresses for Easter. We were doing everything on an equal level as our little brother. So I didn't really have a hard concept of how I would be treated differently. At puberty, my dad started having different expectations and my mom probably did, too, but she didn't talk about them the same way. In my family, there were a lot of women who were equally strong as or stronger than the men in the family. Husbands left for one reason or another, and the women survived. But as I got older, gender got to be more of an issue. At the end of high school, I started playing out a lot musically, and with Emily, of course, we came up against lots of sexism.

J: In what way? Give me some examples.

A: A lack of respect. I had some technical ability to run sound. I'd set up our own sound system, and we'd run it ourselves. We would be sort of scoffed at by the house sound person. It was hard to bring things up on a technical level without getting the man who was in charge of our sound that night mad at us. It was always a man. We never had a sound woman until we hired one ourselves.

J: I remember her! What was her name, again?

A: Michelle Sabolchick. She's worked with Melissa Etheridge, Jewel, Gwen Stefani . . . all those people. Sound men are always touchy with bands, but I felt there was less respect because I was a woman. The promoters were very patronizing. If I put my foot down in order to get paid, the "honeys" and the "babes" came out at that point. All of it was in language and body stance and tone. It's hard to articulate it, because it was so constant that we got used to it and even became numb to it. I just remember we had to work extra hard to get paid what they said they were going to pay. We had to work extra hard to have the sound the way we wanted it. When we were booking our gigs, we were just "two girls with guitars." We had to work extra hard to get respect.

J: What you are describing is the reason that the women's music movement of the early '70s created their own network: their own touring circuit, their own booking, and their own labels, like Olivia Records. They were indie before indie existed. Were you aware of the women's music movement when you first started playing out as a teenager with Emily?

A: When I started playing, in the 1980s, I wasn't aware any movement even happened. I don't even think I knew who [groundbreaking Olivia Records recording artist] Cris Williamson was until '83. That's when I discovered her.

J: Do you remember how you discovered her?

A: I ended up with a couple of records, including *Changer*. I don't remember why. It might have been someone I knew, or my sister. It's pretty vague, because I listened to it a lot but I didn't understand what the context of that record was, the idea of a women-run infrastructure. And even when I heard Ferron a few years later, I didn't understand. I didn't make the connection to the women's bookstore in Atlanta that I went to quite a lot—Charis. I just didn't make the connections.

They would ask us to do these events, and they would say it would be all women. We would be *scared* about it and be like, "Our college frat-boy friends can't come? We can't play it!" When we were at Emory, which was '84 to '86 for me, a lot of our audience was a college audience, so the idea of playing a women's function that was separatist was just scary to us. We acted self-righteous about it, but we were really just scared. I didn't understand the value of it. The musicians that were mentoring us were women playing in Atlanta, and they also had this weird attitude about separatism stuff. They had been really jaded and scared into believing that the reason they weren't getting further was because they had already been categorized as gay women musicians. They wanted to stay as far away from that as possible and not alienate anybody.

J: Is there some truth to being marginalized if you identify too closely with being a gay and/or feminist musician? Or do you think that was just internalized self-hatred?

A: Well, it's internalized self-hatred, but it's also true. If you rise above that self-hatred, you might still be marginalized, because there're so many other people who have self-hatred. More has to change than just you. But the thing about the margins is that there are also fans on the margins. These artists resisted that separatist thing and an audience that would be there for them because they wanted another kind of success, and they didn't get it either.

I think that's the lesson I was learning. That's what I was seeing, and it helped me let go of my fear. Just on a practical level, I was like, "Wow. You're trying not to alienate an audience, but you're alienating another audience." You can't really win. You really just have to play to the people who want to hear you. If that means it's a women's event, then that's what you do. If that's the gig that you get, you do that gig, because you just want your music to be heard and appreciated by somebody.

We got lucky and had a college audience. Things were going really well, and even though we were scared of the gay community and the women's-space-only community, they forgave us and still supported us. We got lucky in their generosity, because we learned our lesson and became politicized.

J: I think it's hard to value the beautiful margin. An infrastructure was created so that you didn't have to deal with sexist sound technicians, but it's hard to value that female-only creation if you don't also feel like you can make it in the mainstream.

A: Everything society says about alternative women-created or queer spaces is so derogatory, it's hard not to take that in and think that it's less. When Emily and I started, we got to reap the benefits of Ferron and June Millington and the Roches being there before us, whether we knew it or not. These were women who were playing their own instruments. That was the big deal, right before us: producers that wouldn't let women play their own guitar parts. I think we can't really appreciate it, because we can't conceive what it would be like to be told systematically that your job was to sing the song; you're not good enough to play your own guitar.

J: What you're describing is era-specific, in a way. In the '80s, not only were you in danger of being marginalized as just having a separatist feminist community for women only, but it was also much more dangerous to be gay and out. How much did it feel like having an all-female crowd also meant risking being out before you were ready?

A: Well, anything associated with separatist space meant gay. No one had the concept that women could be straight and want to be in a separate space for a while. It was hard to separate my internalized homophobia and the external homophobia and misogyny we were really experiencing. The '80s were a time when I had a girlfriend and would go out to gay bars, but my music career was so important to me. I wanted to be accepted by the punk rock community and by a certain songwriter community. None of that was associated with gay. To be out felt like I was risking all of that. I might not get to hang out with Driving and Crying or play the 9:30 Club—things that I really valued artistically. To be aligned with women's music felt like I was risking other communities I needed.

J: Those are terrible choices to have to make.

A: That's the crux of it, too. Not only was I scared and homophobic, I was scared of losing an artistic thread I had. I felt lost in this place where I didn't relate to women's music—what I'd been exposed to, at least—and then it was hard to respect it. I felt like if I gave it its due, I'd be absorbed by that community and lose everything else. It takes a lot of experience to respect the contribution and even the art of this other thing that's so scary, and even be in debt to it. At the same time, you can be developing your own movement for your own generation or community or whatever you define it as.

J: What provoked you to know that it was important for you and Emily to be out lesbian musicians?

A: I just felt like a hypocrite. We had made it pretty big. We were on our second or third record, and we were singing so much about strength and self-esteem and being an individual, believing in yourself. I started to recognize that there was a gay community in our audience. We weren't lying. We didn't ever make up boyfriends or anything like that, but we were skirting the issue. A press request from a gay publication would come, and Emily wouldn't do it. I wanted to come out and Emily didn't. But

I knew I could count on her to feel that way, so sometimes I wondered if I used my loyalty to her to justify not coming out myself.

J: What changed?

A: Emily finally just said something openly at a college-radio press conference in the Northampton/Amherst area. I think they asked her about being gay and she said yes. I just remember a feeling of relief came over me that was huge. Then we realized that our publicist was turning down gay magazines without us knowing.

J: You mean, once you came out, you realized that there had been more of a strategy to dampen your gay profile?

A: Not really a strategy, but it was happening. I would talk to writers at gay publications and they would be like, "Yeah, no one returned our calls." We were being steered away from that constantly. I realized that if we wanted to be out and not be lying in some indirect way, we would have to express that to the label and to our publicist, to say, "We want to do these interviews. It's a community we want to be a part of and it's an audience that's important to us." We had to be very demonstrative about it. It's funny, because now publicists are so desperate to get to any community. They'll say an artist is gay if they have to. [*Laughs.*]

J: Let's talk a little about your evolving relationship with gender. Back when we were dating, we were boarding a plane once and the security guard called you "sir" and you said, "Ma'am!" or, "I'm a woman!" I remember feeling personally destabilized by the exchange, because I really liked that your vibe was very masculine. Yet when there was actual confusion, I felt bad for you: "Oh no! The whole point is that it's supposed to be clear that she's a hot butch woman!" I felt like the worst thing one can possibly do to someone is not grasp his or her gender.

I feel very differently now. I meet people who are trans and make occasional mistakes about chosen pronouns and the like, but I feel like I now am at least conversant. You told me more recently, though, that now you wouldn't feel bad if someone mistook your gender. You would only feel bad for the other person, because they would feel bad.

A: I feel like if someone calls me "sir," they're picking up on who I am, which is, you know, probably more than half male. I probably fall more there. I don't want to lose my 25 percent female, but it is probably only 25 percent.

J: I really do know what you mean, despite your lady parts.

A: Now, I feel pretty comfortable. I think my only struggle is some days waking up in the wrong body and being depressed about it for a few days, but then I get over it, because it's not so much the wrong body that I would change it. It's kind of *mostly* the wrong body, but it's not enough to give it up. When I met you, I was starting to understand my gender. I began to see myself as masculine in a bigger way than I ever had. It was like a door opening, and then it was hanging out with the Butchies and their community and looking at other communities where there was sort of a feminine and masculine dichotomy in a queer relationship that was really obvious—stylistically or attitude-wise. And then understanding that I felt comfortable in that system, where I like to be with someone who's very femme. Then I had to understand that there are a lot of people who feel differently about that, too. It's funny how, with a movement so young, we have to learn definitions and articulate things and have a vocabulary just to move to the next place, but we do. It is the generations after me that are so much better at it.

J: Yes, the young ones. That's who I'm learning from, too! Some people who are concerned about the rise of trans feminism or just

transgenderism in general fear that it serves a misogynist purpose and an anti-gay purpose, too. What do you think about that?

A: I understand what people say about that. Just take the "trans" out, and talk about the part of queer where you feel comfortable in this structure that's almost sort of hetero, because it's a femme/masculine structure. That really probably rose out of the working class, in the very early days of female couples' having to have a way to pass. This is like a structure that passed, in a way. When I understood butch-femme scenes in Seattle or San Francisco or North Carolina, I could see that they were tipping their hat to that era in tattoos—the star on the wrist or the other working-class tattoos—that may have taken it to a different level. They weren't trying to pass in the straight world—feminine or masculine was their aesthetic and their sexuality and how they understand their own kind of hotness. I think it's important to acknowledge the danger of buying into something that's part of the heterosexual world, that has misogyny in it, when you still have to be who you are.

With the trans issue, I understand why people may think there's a tendency towards misogyny or some misogyny mixed in there with trans men—something going on in there about women being seen as less. I know my own struggle with my own body so well. And it's not all misogyny, and it's not all because society told me that women are less or women can't achieve as much, or that I grew up with rock 'n' roll and all my idols were men, so that's what I was taught you have to be to make it. That is *some* of what is going on in my head all the time, but when you feel at odds with your body, it is so much bigger than that political stuff. It's everything you are; it's your core, the way you walk in the world, and when you see someone who's transitioned, who is suddenly *who they are,* it's very powerful.

J: I used to be very anti–plastic surgery, the way you can be when you're twenty-two and have no need for it. But it also just struck me as this sad example of women being taught that they need to do something dangerous in order to remedy how inadequate they are. Then a friend of mine struggled for years to accept the fact that she was entirely flat-chested—not like she has small boobs, but completely flat-chested. Finally, she got breast implants. Now, she looks in the mirror and she sees who she thinks she is. Whereas she used to see kind of a kid—maybe a boy, she wasn't sure—she now sees a woman. She didn't relate internally, in her psyche, to what she was seeing.

A: It's real. Maybe in a hundred years, we'll live in a world where bodies aren't so representational of who we are inside. But, we're not there, and you don't have to live your life as a martyr to that. You do the things that you need to do to feel comfortable with yourself, but at the same time, you work on acceptance, too. Those are two things that can happen at once.

J: **Here's a question that's not about gender: Are you glad you took the major-label route? I know you've always had ambivalence.**

A: Yes, I'm glad.

J: **Why?**

A: They gave us a lot of opportunities. At the time, major labels were still really into developing artists. We were given so many resources—financially, to work in great studios, to work with other artists who were really cool. It's so different now that the concept of what a major label was back then is just foreign to people now. There were a lot of evils associated with it, but they developed bands, and they had a trajectory and long-term plan for you. I probably regret the last few years of it. It was kind of like a bad relationship, where we just didn't get out soon enough.

J: **In what way?**

A: We were getting more and more political; simultaneously, the label just kind of gave up on us because we weren't having hits. They were funneling us into all these radio things for a community that didn't relate to us anymore. Meanwhile, we couldn't tap into a more indie, radical community because we were part of this major-label machinery that does things one dinosaur-ish way.

J: Do you feel like all the independent records you made helped you cycle back around to being part of a radical feminist, separatist community that you originally avoided?

A: Yes, a feminist, queer, separatist community surrounded me when I began doing independent records as Amy Ray. Starting in 2001, I was playing with the Butchies and meeting Le Tigre and Kathleen Hanna and learning so much more about Riot Grrrl. These things were happening on my periphery, but I hadn't been able to connect with them. At the same time, Michigan [Womyn's Music Festival] was getting more radicalized—[punk band] Tribe 8 had played there. It definitely introduced me more to that. The aesthetic of these younger radical feminists was punk, rather than the hippie aesthetic of my youth.

The people I know from doing independent stuff have really been an incredible resource for Indigo Girls. Just so many opportunities and musicians we've met and spaces we've played and other activism opportunities we've had have come from that seed. I feel like it's been invaluable to me and Emily, giving us energy and keeping us on point and interested in what we're doing. The world has changed, but so has the breadth of women's music—and it's now so clearly where I want to be.

—Interviewed on February 24, 2011

TAKE BACK THE NIGHT.
AGAIN.

It might have been at the University of Wisconsin-Madison or the University of Delaware or even Miami University, which is, oddly, in Oxford, Ohio. I was very likely surrounded by young students, men and women, carrying hand-lettered signs and sheets decorated with women symbols. I was most certainly *verklempt,* as I always am at Take Back the Night marches—emotional to be among the vibrant crowd, to see how many people care about the safety of women, humbled to be among so many who have been raped, incested, or molested. But I also felt a nagging sense of déjà vu, a Groundhog Day kind of dread that this particular Take Back the Night was just like the one I went to in 1989 at my own college. I couldn't help but wonder, with increasing sadness, will Skuli and Magnus also be attending Take Back the Nights at their future colleges? Will women ever feel like the night is ours?

I acknowledge that we've made progress. In fact, by the time the first Take Back the Night march was held in San Francisco in 1978, feminists had already made several major contributions to eradicating sexual assault. Authors such as Susan Brownmiller made rape visible, revealing its long history and rescuing it from the realm of a bad date that was somehow your fault. She, and others, placed sexual assault where it rightly belongs—within the domain of crime. For the first time, women used the word rape to describe nonconsensual sex when the aggressor was a husband, a date, or a friend. They connected rape to the systematic oppression of women under patriarchy. Brownmiller famously wrote: "From prehistoric times to the present, I believe, rape has played a critical function. It is nothing more or less than a conscious process of intimidation by which *all men* keep *all women* in a state of fear" (italics hers).[1]

Brownmiller's indicting statement reflects feminism's second major contribution. The creators of the women's liberation movement attempted to untangle rape from the dizzying array of other factors surrounding it—alcohol, outfits, past experiences, reputations—and distill it to its essence. They created maxims such as "rape is about power, not sex" and "no means no."

One of the most important things I learned as I came into my own as a feminist is that no matter how profound and groundbreaking the insight, strategies must evolve in order to push the feminist agenda further. Younger people might build on what came before—as Jaclyn Friedman and Jessica Valenti did with their anti-rape anthology *Yes Means Yes*—or they might have to get rid of it altogether. Doing Take Back the Night year after year is fine as a tradition and a celebration but is a sideline, perhaps, to actually deepening our understanding of and ability to eradicate rape. Take Back the Night doesn't function as it once did. If our objective is to

---

1. Brownmiller, Susan. *Against Our Will: Men, Women and Rape* (New York: Ballantine Books, 1975).

reduce the number of rapes to zero, to move beyond analysis and protest and into actions, what might they be?

One solution is to break the original silences that swirl around women's bodies. Peter Vincent D'Angelo (a.k.a. Vinnie Angel) grew up in the 1970s. His family was Italian/Irish, traditional (stay-at-home mom, professor dad), and all boys. His mom presumably menstruated, but he didn't really know, because she never made an effort to explain it to them. Meanwhile, TV and magazine ads overtly sold women and men on the idea of silence. As such, Vinnie learned that a successful period to a girl or woman is one in which no one knows she's having it. In order to be polite and support girls in their quest to have invisible, mysterious periods, he never let on that he knew his high school and college girlfriends were on the rag.

Many years later, out of college and working as an artist in New York City, Vinnie decided to make an experimental film in which he asked a bunch of his friends the same vapid twenty questions a reporter had asked Magic Johnson in an old issue of *Sporting News* magazine. One of the questions was "What is the worst thing that has ever happened to you?" Vinnie filmed a female friend, and when he got to that question, she said, breaking into tears, "I guess when I was gang-raped in high school and when I tried to talk about it, no one believed me."

Vinnie was flabbergasted. He couldn't believe he'd known this friend so intimately and for such a long time and yet had never known about this major trauma in her life. He thought of the silencing she must have felt, and his mind skipped to the other ways in which women are told to stay silent and invisible about what happens to them. He wanted to respond to this gross injustice, but he wasn't sure how to get to the root of something so awful. And then it came to him: He was going to create a tampon case and it was going to be red and black and tough looking (no pink and lavender euphemisms for this scabbard). He—a man—was going to give away ten thousand of these cases and allow this seemingly innocuous canvas tampon case placed in backpacks, pockets, and purses, to inspire spontaneous conversations between women and men about menstruation and the realities of women's bodies. Fifteen years later, in 2011, more than half a million women around the world use his tampon cases—each case representing a leap, however small, into talking about what happens to women "down there."

Vinnie's friend's experience points to how upside down our approach to rape still is. If you are raped, you descend down a rabbit hole into a parallel world where getting hurt means that you, and probably only you, will be punished. Even the signs and programs meant to address the problem underscore that it's mainly women's behavior that we are trying to control. But what if our behavior modification were directed not at victims, but at perpetrators? A subway ad in New York City proclaims: YOU DON'T HAVE TO ACCEPT SEXUAL HARASSMENT. SAY NO! REPORT IT! An enterprising designer could slap a poster over that which says: DON'T ABUSE OR SEXUALLY HARASS ANYONE! IF YOU DO, YOU ARE DISGUSTING AND YOU WILL BE PUNISHED!" In addition to teaching kids about good and bad touches, we could meet sitters at the door and say, "Bedtime is at eight; make sure he uses the bathroom before bed. Am I forgetting anything? Oh, yes, and definitely *don't* molest my child."

Speaking out, a staple of Take Back the Night marches, still has its place—primarily in terms of providing a sense of support and community for people who have been raped, and for creating space to name what has happened to so many. I've interviewed dozens of women and a couple of men about their rape stories, and each is uniquely heartbreaking and shattering and provides a crucial sense that rape victims are not alone. Still, these accounts aren't necessarily useful for prevention.

As I travel to college campuses, I'm struck by how much awkwardness there is around sex, and how alcohol and drugs are used to quell uncomfortable feelings of gracelessness and embarrassment. What's needed, of course, is honest, direct, and somewhat sober communication among people before the rape occurs. Ben Privot, a 2010 graduate of Drew University, created the Consensual Project, which brings to colleges workshops that make consent understandable and, he hopes, sexy. Privot aligns with younger feminist organizations, such as PAVE (Promoting Awareness, Victim Empowerment), and groups that focus on male behavior, such as Men Can Stop Rape.

Men are becoming more powerful as anti-rape activists—not just by talking to other men about behavior that might be unsafe for women, but also by telling the truth about their own experiences of rape. David Benzaquen, the political and legislative action coordinator for NARAL Pro-Choice New York, is a survivor of rape—in his case a sexual assault by his girlfriend when he was 18. Men like David who are brave enough to come out about their own sexual assaults provide crucial insight into the psychology of rape—especially why a person who, theoretically, appears strong enough to get away from an attacker can't.

Feminists of all stripes are providing ideas to prevent rape, too. In 2004, musician Oraia Reid was outraged by a surge in sexual assaults targeting women walking home at night in North Brooklyn. She founded RightRides, which uses volunteers (working in groups of two) and Zipcars to provide free rides home for women and LGBTQ individuals. The organization's tagline is "Getting home safely shouldn't be a luxury." In 2005, Emily May founded Hollaback!, "a movement dedicated to ending street harassment" by encouraging would-be victims to record their harasser on their phone and send the recording to the Hollaback! website, thus publicizing what women's silence often protects.

The other day, my ultra-organized friend Constance looked over my list of ongoing projects to help me prioritize my life. She wrote down each project or job obligation on an index card and then made three piles: immediate, two months from now, and no deadline. She looked at the card listing my rape awareness project called It Was Rape, composed of a film in postproduction, a T-shirt, and resource cards. She paused, then snapped it down authoritatively onto the no-deadline pile. "That one is evergreen," she said as I protested meekly. "Rape is an ongoing problem that, sadly, will be there when you get to it."

Armed with my cell phone and my tampon case, I'm hearing stories about women raping and men being raped, continuing to evolve an understanding of this common, silenced experience. The problem of rape persists—it overwhelms—but the crews of feminists I see taking an individual interest in everyone's safety makes me feel like someone really *is* taking back the night. And also seizing the day, the subways, and the movement. I say to all of you Slutwalkers, Knightriders, and Hollabackers, "Don't you stop."

A WOMAN IN THE WHITE HOUSE

I grew up in the kind of Midwestern small-town household in which my mother stayed at home with us kids, dealing with meals, laundry, cleaning, and volunteer work, while my father worked as a doctor and was the more authoritative disciplinarian. We were three daughters, though, and while our family was superficially traditional, we were fed a steady diet of "you can be whatever you want." That meant, to be honest, "you can do what boys do" more than it was an invitation to also become full-time homemakers.

At age seven or so, I remember musing that I might become "a fashion designer or a nurse" when I grew up, and my mother's responding, a bit too intensely, "Or a doctor. You don't have to be a nurse. Women can be doctors!" Her adamancy came not from any contempt for nurses—her own mother, my grandma Effie, had sent three kids to college and helped countless people in Grand Forks, North Dakota, as an RN. No, the intensity with which she begged me to consider the more publicly valued work came from her own biography.

Growing up, she got the impression that there were two jobs for women: nurse or teacher. Once she got a glimpse, during the 1970s, of the vastness of the world women might have access to, she felt a bit rooked. She got her master's degree, writing her thesis on the life of Billie Holliday, and also invested many of her hopes in seeing what her daughters would do. Like many of her generation, she lived (consciously or not) the mantra that she would be the root and her daughters the bloom. Meanwhile, although she was proud of the work she did raising us kids and running the household, she knew that until women occupied the spaces men had always called solely theirs, it would be hard to argue that we were "just choosing" to become homemakers or nurses or any "helping professional."

I thought a lot about my mother's dream that her daughters—and thus women—would continue to demonstrate that they were as good as men while I observed the 2008 presidential candidacy of Senator Hillary Clinton. She was not the first woman to run—from Belva Lockwood (1884 and 1888) to Brooklyn Congresswoman Shirley Chisholm (1972) to Illinois Senator Carol Moseley Braun (2004), we've had a handful of women gutsy enough to go for the top job—but HRC is *by far* the most serious contender, as demonstrated by the infrastructure and money she was quickly able to attract. Like Oprah and Madonna, she had 100 percent name recognition (a crucial element in politics), but unlike them, she had cowritten and sponsored important legislation, was a very successful two-term senator from a huge state, spoke of women's rights as human rights at the Fourth World Conference on Women in Beijing in 1995 (the first time that seemingly obvious observation was made in a way that could affect policy), and blocked the confirmation of the FDA commissioner to protest the long delay in approving

Plan B for over-the-counter use. During the primaries, she created the most detailed and only truly universal healthcare proposal put before the voters—something similar to the plan Obama passed after becoming president.

The reasons people gave for not supporting Clinton ranged from her war authorization vote to fear that her husband would dominate the rest of the election cycle or the White House, but what I heard more was the fact that she's just not "electable" because, as some said, wrinkling their noses, "she's not likable." Creating this self-fulfilling prophecy, the media piled on, chalking up sixty-two major incidents of egregious misogyny in fewer than six months leading up to the election, according to a tally of anti-Hillary sexist episodes in the primary-campaign compiles by Melissa McEwan. As Stan Fish wrote on his *New York Times* blog, to mention her name is to prompt an archive more of vitriol than substantive criticism, most of it reflecting a frightening level of woman hating.

At my Brooklyn polling place on Super Tuesday, I unambivalently—proudly!—voted for Hillary Clinton. As I left the building, my eyes pricked with tears and a wave of emotion swept over me. I'm often moved by voting (is it the barely conscious realization that women went on hunger strikes not even a century ago so I could have that right?). I cried when I voted for John Kerry, and I wasn't even that enthused about him as a candidate. But February 5, 2008, was different. It was a big deal to me, at age thirty-seven, to pull the lever for a woman who so clearly had what it takes. More than that, Hillary Clinton had endured the attacks and derision we all know happen when women step out of line. She had become a sort of martyr-feminist, putting herself out there at great personal cost to provide some reality behind our "free to be . . . you and me" rhetoric.

I spoke with other friends who also reported being utterly

choked up. "I have devoted forty years—practically my entire adult life—to bringing about this possibility, this fulfillment of what seemed an unattainable dream," an older friend wrote me in an email. "It's hard for me to understand those feminists who are voting for an unknown quantity instead of her, when they have this chance of a lifetime. Especially since the rivals' positions are so similar." Other women recounted voting for Obama, then feeling surprised at how happy they were that Hillary did well on Super Tuesday. "I felt it would be selfish to vote for her," another friend told me.

At the height of the historic presidential election of 2008, a bitter reality began to sink in for me, a daughter of the Second Wave, and even sink me a bit. There we were, several generations who were raised with the mantra that a "woman" could be president, learning that it didn't mean any woman who actually existed.

Barack Obama is clearly a feminist-minded man who shares little with traditional rules of masculinity or the typical biography of a president. He is biracial, was raised by a white single mother, scarcely knew his father, and never served in the military. He married a powerful woman who made more money than he for many years. He is bookish and literary, doesn't profess to hunt, and is the doting, hands-on father to two girls. When he was inaugurated as the forty-fourth president, I felt proud of America. What a leap forward it was for a nation still wrestling with the trauma of our slavery-based past. Having him achieve this office, even when Hillary didn't, salved the pain I felt from knowing that the crimes against women in the United States are many and often invisible. We aren't ready for women who dare to be both mothers and people, for a woman whose ambition is direct—and so unseemly.

Hillary Clinton is my mother's age. What might it have meant for a woman of her generation to achieve what we all assumed would go to her daughter's generation? Sometimes I wonder if the pain of those missed opportunities—of wondering what could have been accomplished if a woman had simply been selfish and not submerged her hopes in her daughters or lived in a different time—was behind some of the commitment to making sure we don't have a woman in the White House, except as First Lady.

IS THERE A FOURTH WAVE?
DOES IT MATTER?

The people who were part of what is often called the First Wave of feminism in the United States didn't identify as "First Wavers." That designation was applied to the suffragists retroactively after a second swell of activism by American women occurred, in the 1960s and 1970s. Martha Lear, a journalist, is credited with coining the term "second feminist wave" in her 1968 article about the women's liberation movement for *The New York Times Sunday Magazine*. Active feminists at the time considered themselves part of that movement, preferring that association to the term "feminist."

After the backlash of the 1980s, women my age got interested in and active in women's rights on their own behalf. In 1990, writer Rebecca Walker—daughter of poet Alice Walker and exactly my age—wrote that our generation was not full of postfeminist feminists (the slur that had appeared in another *New York Times Sunday Magazine* article); we were "the Third Wave." Her term sounded good to the several cofounders of the Third Wave Foundation

(Walker included) and to scads of younger academics, activists, and feminists, and it sounded good to me. It was both connected to and different from what had come before, I thought—and still think.

Of course, not everyone agrees. Within feminism, many find the concept of waves deeply flawed and annoying. "I don't know who Martha Lear is," Roxanne Dunbar-Ortiz, a professor and cofounder of the Boston separatist feminist group Cell 16 in the late 1960s, told me, "but I'd like to give her a piece of my mind for inventing that ahistorical and politically reactionary moniker." The journalist Susan Faludi pointed out that she is chronologically between the two waves but temperamentally skews toward the Second Wave. Eve Ensler, who is chronologically Second Wave and came of age in that movement, calls her sensibility Third Wave because she's committed to being funny and sexy and she uses art and pop culture to create her movement. Certainly, Eve's most profound contributions to feminism—*The Vagina Monologues* and V-Day—are powered by Third Wave feminists who have performed her play on college campuses and around the world for the last decade. Feminists twenty years younger than I am don't fit easily into my era's identification with Nirvana, Riot Grrrls, and abortion rights marches in spite of the fact that no backlash has corrupted our wave. Meanwhile, I don't understand an adolescence with abstinence-only education, purity rings, and Livejournal. And where to put bell hooks, the 1970s feminist who is also the most significant influence on Third Wave college students and Riot Grrrls?

If you think too hard about the criteria for each label, the integrity of the waves disintegrates rapidly and they eddy into one another, the way ocean waves do. But if anyone is going to resist a new wave, it is the previous wave, populated by women and men who believe that they have plenty left to offer and don't need to be put out to sea. Ednie Kaeh Garrison recast this metaphor as radio waves, rather than ocean waves, in a 2000 essay, to convey that feminism's reach was growing with each wave, moving further away (in time and in sheer numbers) from the small band of women who came together in 1848 for the first women's rights convention on U.S. soil—the Seneca Falls Convention.

Garrison believes that the waves are bound to historical cultural moment but don't necessarily define a cohort of feminists by age. "The 'third' is the mark of historical specificity, and like the marker 'second' in the Second Wave, it is not simply a sign of generational descendence," she writes. "When we automatically assume 'third' refers to a specific generation, we actually erase the significant presence and contributions of many overlapping and multiple cohorts who count as feminists, and more particularly, of those who can count as Third Wave feminists."[1]

Personally, I find the waves useful shorthand in describing the broad strokes of feminist history, which most people don't know in even the most cursory way, much less a nuanced one. The American history we get in schoolbooks is also condensed, politically retrograde, and filled with holes—yet it at least provides the barest frame to view where we have been and where we are going. Feminism needs that same road map. We can add to it, balk at it, revel in it—but first we have to have it. What follows is a really, really short history of feminism.

WAVE ZERO

More than five hundred years before the Seneca Falls women's liberation meeting in 1848, on the piece of land that would come to be called the United States, Iroquois and Cherokee clan mothers decided who would be chief and created war strategy, boys and

---

1. Garrison, Ednie Kaeh. "U.S. Feminism—Grrrl Style! Youth (Sub)Cultures and the Technologics of the Third Wave." *Feminist Studies* 26 (spring 2000), 141–70.

girls were given an equal education, and women had control over their fertility and children. Many of the nearly five hundred Native American tribes thriving at the time provided an example of egalitarian society that the accidental arrival of Christopher Columbus would later obliterate.

In 1405, Parisian scholar Christine de Pisan published *The Book of the City of Ladies* in France. She argued that throughout history, women who had challenged the patriarchy had ruled in France and expressed the right and desire of women to be treated as fully human—that is, capable of being ambitious, intellectual, brave, or opportunistic. In Britain in 1792, Mary Wollstonecraft published *A Vindication of the Rights of Women*, a foundational feminist work that says women aren't intellectually inferior to men but their lack of access to education and other resources stunts their development.

THE FIRST WAVE (APPROXIMATELY 1840-1920)

The First Wave grew out of the movement to abolish slavery. That movement, and the ensuing one dedicated to women's rights, drew from the ideals and disappointments of the new democracy. These Americans, many of them Quakers, believed that it was their moral responsibility to oppose slavery. The women who were active in this movement soon discovered that they, as females, didn't have the rights that they were agitating for black men to have. As just one example, many women traveled with their husbands across the Atlantic to a historic abolitionist conference in London, only to be barred from entering once they arrived. They applied their raised consciousness, organizing skills, and philosophical template to themselves and fought this exclusion. Their strategies and technology included creating the Declaration of Sentiments (based on the Declaration of Independence, but including women), making speeches, writing books, and organizing marches.

If the First Wave had to be boiled down to one goal, it was rights of citizenship. The most important symbol of citizenship in a democracy is the right to vote, which suffragists asked for in July 1848, to universal ridicule, and achieved seventy-two years and one month later, on August 20, 1920. En route to the vote, these feminists changed our culture, shepherding in dress reform, birth control, and granting to women the right to own property, get divorced, be educated, keep their income and inheritance, and retain custody of their children. Alice Paul, a crucial organizer for women's suffrage, quickly identified that a vote in such an unequal nation was less powerful than it could or should be. In 1923, she introduced the Lucretia Mott Amendment, also known as the Equal Rights Amendment, or ERA.

THE SECOND WAVE (APPROXIMATELY 1960–1988)

Like the First Wave, the Second Wave grew out of an enormous social justice movement—the civil rights movement, which was reaching its apex in the early 1960s. Young people of all races flocked to the movement, eager to be a part of finishing the work of ensuring rights to black Americans. Once again, women in this movement—as well as the peace, free speech, and gay rights movements—found that they themselves didn't have the rights that they were agitating for on behalf of others. They turned their raised consciousness and organizing skills on themselves and created an independent women's liberation movement (the preferred term of this band of feminists). The radical feminists of this era believed in full-scale revolution for the common good. The liberal feminists fought for women to share in the opportunities and responsibilities men had, including creating a career, pushing off the drudgery of housework, and refusing to be held hostage by their reproductive systems.

The dominant goal of these feminists might be boiled down to equality—valuing equally that which was marked as female or feminine, such as knitting or childbirth, and having equal access to domains that had been exclusive to men. Second Wave feminists demonstrated that, given the opportunity or necessity, women could do what men did. They also made women's activities visible and valuable. Their core beliefs stemmed from Marx, identifying women as an oppressed class and patriarchy as the illegitimate power over them. These feminists declared that *they* were the experts—not male doctors, shrinks, religious leaders, fathers, or husbands—when it came to abortion, rape, pregnancy, and female sexuality. They created language and resources for atrocities once just called "life"—such as date rape, domestic abuse, and illegal abortion. They lobbied for laws and court decisions to strike down legal inequality, such as Title IX, the Equal Pay Act, and *Roe v. Wade*.

By the mid-1980s, the concept of women as a class with overarching shared values and experiences was deeply splintered. Black women, women with disabilities, Latinas, lesbian and bisexual women, and others began critiquing the broad philosophies of the movement from within, causing splits that were rife with both tension and detailed feminist theory. The Combahee River Collective, a black feminist lesbian group that included Barbara Smith and Alexis De Veaux, created the theory of "interlocking oppressions." This necessary deepening and expanding of feminist definitions coincided with a general backlash against feminism by people who wanted to undo the gains of the Second Wave.

THE THIRD WAVE (APPROXIMATELY 1988–2010)

The Third Wave grew out of an enormous cultural shift. By the late 1980s, a cohort of women and men who'd been raised with the gains, theories, flaws, and backlash of the feminist movement were beginning to come of age. Whether or not these individual men and women were raised by self-described feminists— or called themselves feminists—they were living feminist lives: Females were playing sports and running marathons, taking charge of their sex lives, being educated in greater numbers than men, running for office, and working outside the home. For those who were consciously feminist, the splits of the 1980s formed the architecture of their theories. Kimberlé Crenshaw's description of "intersectionality" drew on the work of the Combahee River Collective and advanced the idea that gender might be just one of many entry points for feminism.

The Third Wave rejected the idea of a shared political priority list or even a set of issues one must espouse to be feminist. It inherited critiques of sexist dominant culture (having grown up in a feminist-influenced civilization) and embraced and created pop culture that supported women, from Queen Latifah to bell hooks to Riot Grrrl. Girlie feminists created magazines and fashion statements (and complicated the idea of what a feminist might look like). Sex positivity undermined the notion that porn and sex work are inherently demeaning, and revealed a glimpse of the range of potential sexual expression.

Trans feminism, both the idea (from Judith Butler) that gender is performed and the belief that gender exists on a spectrum, complicated the legitimacy of women-only spaces as sites of unadulterated liberation. Reclaiming words like "slut" and "girl" replaced protests. Transparency about whether a feminist had worked out her body image issues, felt upset by an abortion, or believed that any hair could be unwanted replaced strong, black-and-white statements. Activists spoke from personal places, not to overshare, but to tell the truth about their lives and what had happened to them.

Third Wave feminism was portable—you didn't have to go to a meeting to be feminist; you could bring feminism into any room you entered. Where the Second Wave radicals believed in mass movement and the liberal feminists believed in creating women's institutions to influence men's, a Third Waver might say, "Every time I move, I make a women's movement,"[1] indicating a feminism that is more individually driven. Institutions like NOW and *Ms.* magazine attenuated, in part because Third Wave feminists didn't need any members to be feminist. And while they were committed to a pro-girl and pro-woman line, that didn't preclude empathy for or interest in men's experience of, for instance, sexual assault or abortion.

THE FOURTH WAVE (APPROXIMATELY 2008–ONWARD!)

By the time Obama and Hillary were facing off in the Democratic primaries, a critical mass of younger feminists began expressing themselves. They were tech-savvy and gender-sophisticated. Their youth was shaped by the 1980s backlash, Take Our Daughters to Work Day initiatives (also knows as the Girls' Movement, led by Second Wave women) of the '90s, and 9/11. Perhaps most significant, though, their experience of the online universe was that it was just a part of life, not something that landed in their world like an alien spaceship when they were twenty or fifty.

Much like the Third Wave lived out the theories of the Second Wave (with sometimes surprising results), the Fourth Wave enacted the concepts that Third Wave feminists had put forth. The Doula Project made sure the phrase "all-options" was more than just rhetoric, by creating doula services not just for childbirth, but for women placing an adoption or getting an abortion, too. Drawing from their own experiences, young activists created after-abortion talk lines,

---

1. From Ani DiFranco's song "Hour Follows Hour."

such as Exhale and Backline, to enable women and men to get the support they needed after a procedure—no enforced political line included. Trans-health initiatives (like that at the Feminist Women's Health Centers in Atlanta) and trans-inclusive organizations like Third Wave Foundation (helmed by feminists in their twenties and thirties) reinforced the potential for all people to access feminine and masculine genders.

In place of zines and songs, young feminists created blogs, Twitter campaigns, and online media with names like Racialicious and Feministing, or wrote for Jezebel and Salon's Broadsheet. They commented on the news, posted their most stylish plus-size fashion photos with info about where to shop, and tweeted that they, too, had had an abortion. "Reproductive justice," coined by women of color in the 1990s, became the term of choice for young feminists. Transgenderism, male feminists, sex work, and complex relationships within the media characterized their feminism.

WHAT DO ALL of these waves add up to? Some analyze the era-specific crests of feminism as merely more splits, keeping feminists fighting with one another so that they don't see the much larger and more challenging issues that unite them. A Second Wave friend of mine, Rosalyn Baxandall, notes that the First and Second Waves were part of larger social movements—abolition and civil rights—and were thus different than the trickles of activity she sees as having come later. But I see the cultural transformation that my generation harvested from the Second Wave's ideas and revolution was the social movement of our day. Likewise, the Fourth Wave's deployment of social media has once again transformed politics and feminism.

Personally, I believe that the Fourth Wave exists because it says that it exists. I believe the Fourth Wave matters, because I remember how sure I was that my generation mattered.

Because of media advances and globalization, waves of mass change are coming faster and faster. The waves are all part of the same body politic known as feminism, and combine to become a powerful and distinct force. "One aspect of the 'waves' metaphor that I kinda like," the historian Louise Bernikow wrote on our Second Wave–dominated LISTSERV, "is the idea that waves recede and gather strength and come back stronger, don't they?"

"Tsunami!" replied Roxanne Dunbar-Ortiz, the professor who resented Martha Lear's coinage of "Second Wave." "Let's do it."

ACKNOWLEDGMENTS

I'm gaga over the many people who helped me with this book. Many thanks to Sarah Nager, Tara Storozynsky, Jessica Baumgardner, Anastasia Higginbotham, and Gretchen Sayers for editing and other supportive gestures. My deepest appreciation to Cathi Hanauer, Ada Calhoun, Ellen Seidman, and Kim Cutter for skillful original editing of the reprinted essays in this book. I'm grateful to Kathleen Hanna, Amy Ray, Ani DiFranco, Julia Serano, Björk, Loretta Ross, Shelby Knox, and Debbie Stoller for their time and insightful interviews. Finally, thank you to Merrik Bush-Pirkle for thoughtful, supportive, and sensitive guidance throughout the editorial process, and to Jill Grinberg, for being a super agent and friend.

My life while writing this book was enriched immeasurably by Gretchen Sayers, Anastasia Higginbotham, Jessica and Andrea (plus families), Mom and Dad, and my favorite feminists, the Bedbaums.

PHOTO CREDITS

ABOUT THE AUTHOR

Writer and activist Jennifer Baumgardner is the author of *Look Both Ways: Bisexual Politics* and *Abortion & Life*, and the coauthor, with Amy Richards, of *Manifesta: Young Women, Feminism, and the Future,* and *Grassroots: A Field Guide for Feminist Activism.* As coowner of the feminist speakers' bureau Soapbox, Inc., Baumgardner runs Feminist Summer Camp and Feminist Winter Term in New York with Richards, and she has lectured at more than three hundred schools. She writes for *Glamour, The Nation, Real Simple,* and *Babble,* among other publications, and is the producer of the award-winning documentary *I Had an Abortion,* and of a forthcoming film about rape. A teacher at The New School, she lives in New York City with her husband and two sons.

SELECTED TITLES FROM SEAL PRESS

For more than thirty years, Seal Press has published
groundbreaking books. By women. For women.

We Don't Need Another Wave: Dispatches from the Next Generation of Feminists, edited by Melody Berger. $15.95, 978-1-58005-182-8. In the tradition of Listen Up, the under-thirty generation of young feminists speaks out.

Yes Means Yes: Visions of Female Sexual Power and A World Without Rape, by Jaclyn Friedman and Jessica Valenti. $16.95, 978-1-58005-257-3. This powerful and revolutionary anthology offers a paradigm shift from the "No Means No" model, challenging men and women to truly value female sexuality and ultimately end rape.

What You Really Really Want: The Smart Girl's Shame-Free Guide to Sex and Safety, by Jaclyn Friedman. $17.00, 978-1-58005-344-0. An educational and interactive guide that gives young women the tools they need to decipher the modern world's confusing, hypersexualized landscape and define their own sexual identity.

Girldrive: Criss-Crossing America, Redefining Feminism, by Nona Willis Aronowitz and Emma Bee Bernstein. $19.95, 978-1-58005-273-3. Two young women set out on the open road to explore the current state of feminism in the US.

Gender Outlaws: The Next Generation, edited by Kate Bornstein and S. Bear Bergman. $16.95, 978-1-58005-308-2. Collects and contextualizes the work of this generation's trans and genderqueer forward-thinkers—new voices from the stage, on the streets, in the workplace, in the bedroom, and on the pages and websites of the world's most respected news sources.

Click: When We Knew We Were Feminists, edited by Courtney E. Martin and J. Courtney Sullivan. $16.95, 978-1-58005-285-6. Notable writers and celebrities entertain and illuminate with true stories recalling the distinct moments when they knew they were feminists.

FIND SEAL PRESS ONLINE

www.SealPress.com
www.Facebook.com/SealPress
Twitter: @SealPress